THE NARRATIVE OF ANTONIO MUÑOZ MOLINA

Currents in Comparative Romance Languages and Literatures

Tamara Alvarez-Detrell and Michael G. Paulson
General Editors

Vol. 78

PETER LANG
New York • Washington, D.C./Baltimore • Boston
Bern • Frankfurt am Main • Berlin • Vienna • Paris

Lawrence Rich

THE NARRATIVE OF ANTONIO MUÑOZ MOLINA

Self-Conscious Realism and "El Desencanto"

PETER LANG
New York • Washington, D.C./Baltimore • Boston
Bern • Frankfurt am Main • Berlin • Vienna • Paris

Library of Congress Cataloging-in-Publication Data

Rich, Lawrence.
The narrative of Antonio Muñoz Molina:
self-conscious realism and "el desencanto" / by Lawrence Rich.
p. cm. — (Currents in comparative Romance languages and literatures; vol. 78)
Includes bibliographical references (p. –) and index.
1. Muñoz Molina, Antonio—Criticism and interpretation. I. Title. II. Series:
Currents in comparative Romance languages and literatures; vol. 78.
PQ6663.U4795Z85   863'.64—dc21   98-4951
ISBN 0-8204-4080-9
ISSN 0893-5963

Die Deutsche Bibliothek-CIP-Einheitsaufnahme

Rich, Lawrence:
The narrative of Antonio Muñoz Molina:
self-conscious realism and "El desencanto" / Lawrence Rich.
–New York; Washington, D.C./Baltimore; Boston; Bern;
Frankfurt am Main; Berlin; Vienna; Paris: Lang.
(Currents in comparative Romance languages
and literatures; Vol. 78)
ISBN 0-8204-4080-9

Permission for passages from Wolfgang Iser's
The Act of Reading: A Theory of Aesthetic Response (1978)
and *The Implied Reader: Patterns of Communication in Prose from Bunyan
to Beckett* (1974) were granted by The Johns Hopkins University Press

Author photo © by Celia Escudero-Espadas

The paper in this book meets the guidelines for permanence and durability
of the Committee on Production Guidelines for Book Longevity
of the Council of Library Resources.

© 1999 Lawrence Rich

All rights reserved.
Reprint or reproduction, even partially, in all forms such as microfilm,
xerography, microfiche, microcard, and offset strictly prohibited.

Printed in the United States of America

Dedication

To Celia and Rubén for their patience

To Doris and Stanley for their support

To Victoria and Antonio for their trust

To Antonio Muñoz Molina for his artistry

Acknowledgements

A book is always a collaborative effort, and I owe my deepest thanks to a number of people, including:

José María Naharro-Calderón, who first suggested that I study the work of Antonio Muñoz Molina.

Carmen Benito-Vessels, who introduced me to the exciting world of literary theory and historiography.

Chad Wright, whose invaluable scholarly criticism and advice were accompanied by a warmth and friendship I will never forget.

Amrita Kaur, Suvarna Francis, Chris Winters, Patricia Brody and Terry Sayler at the University of Maryland's McKeldin Library.

The committee members of the Program for Cultural Cooperation Between Spain's Ministry of Culture and United States' Universities, for a research grant which allowed me to spend a month at the *Hemeroteca Nacional* in Madrid.

Chris Rich, for her superb proofreading.

Elaine Thompson, for her diligent production.

Antonio Muñoz Molina, who granted me the time to interview him on two occasions and permitted me to cite from his works.

All passages from Narrative Fiction: Contemporary Poetics © *1983 by Shlomith Rimmon-Kenan are printed with the permission of Routledge, Ltd.*

TABLE OF CONTENTS

Preface xi

Introduction 1

Chapter 1. Mixing Memory and Imagination 11

Chapter 2. History and Metafiction 35

Chapter 3. Engaging the Reader 57

Chapter 4. Intertextualing the Popular 77

Chapter 5. Self-Conscious Realism and the
 (Auto)biographical Mode 95

Conclusion. "El Desencanto" 111

Bibliography 119

Index 131

Preface

Antonio Muñoz Molina is presently one of Spain's most popular and widely-read authors. His novels and short stories have been translated into a number of modern languages, and many of them are now part of the literary canon of the post-Franco era. Yet surprisingly there have been few comprehensive critical studies of his narrative. This book is an attempt to answer that lack.

When I began writing, Muñoz Molina criticism consisted of a handful of articles and a 1992 doctoral dissertation by Francisco García-Moreno Barco, a valuable work that relies heavily on postmodernist theory. I share García-Moreno's belief that unstable political and economic conditions during the Spanish political transition after Franco's death can account for certain "postmodern" phenomena—in particular the challenge to literary elitism and a turn to popular genres such as the crime novel. However, I feel that it is dangerous to assign postmodernism, as Moreno-García does, to a periodizing category ("El posmodernismo aparece tras el colapso de 1973" [66]). And while I fully agree with him that Muñoz Molina posits "la imposibilidad de conocimiento" (82), one may argue, as does Brian McHale, that epistemological concerns are also characteristic of modernist writers (*Postmodernist Fiction* 9–10). Malcolm Compitello has joined other critics who have questioned the use of the term "postmodernism," stating that

> a...lack of clarity abounds in the way the term postmodernism is used in describing the current intellectual environment in Spain. This is what leads me to affirm that there is no Spanish postmodernism, or in less polemical terms, that there is no need to use this term when speaking to current cultural events in Spain. ("Benet and Spanish Postmodernism" 268–69)

Consequently, throughout this study I have tried to avoid whenever possible the term "postmodernism." Instead, I have chosen to examine Muñoz Molina's narrative through five closely related theoretical lenses:

narratology, metafiction, reader response and reception, intertextuality and autobiography. I am well aware that I could have employed other theoretical models, but I am confident that future critics will provide additional insights into Muñoz Molina's work from perspectives other than my own. My recent experience teaching a course on Hispanic women's literature has convinced me that a feminist critique of male post-Franco authors is long overdue, and Silvia Bermúdez's article "Negro que te quiero rosa: La feminización de la novela de espías en *Beltenebros*," which appeared in 1994 in *España contemporánea*, is an encouraging indicator of future Muñoz Molina criticism. For those readers who may take me to task for the absence of a feminist critique, my only justification is that such an undertaking would have produced a very different book, one which I was simply not prepared to write at the time.

Muñoz Molina's last two novels, *Ardor guerrero* (1995) and *Plenilunio* (1997), appeared after I had completed the first version of this study. Although I have not discussed the latter novel, a brief comment on the former is in order. Unlike *El jinete polaco* and *El dueño del secreto*, *Ardor guerrero* presents itself as a non-fictional autobiographical memoir of the author's experiences as a military recruit. However, despite its humorous touches, it ends on the same note of disillusionment that I find characteristic of Muñoz Molina's previous works. The author-narrator discovers that one of his closest friends—not coincidentally a leftist militant intent on changing Spain through revolutionary means—has died in a car crash.

La voz narrativa de Antonio Muñoz Molina by Manuel María Morales Cuesta (Barcelona: Octaedro, 1996) only recently came to my attention. Morales Cuesta notes that he tried to avoid "un excesivo academicismo" (13), and his book is indeed an excellent review of Muñoz Molina's narrative aimed towards non-academic readers. In contrast, my study is intended for a variety of academically-oriented readers, including professors of Spanish or Comparative Literature and both graduate and advanced undergraduate students. Professors may refer to it for their teaching and research needs, and students will also find it useful as an introduction to contemporary theories of literature.

INTRODUCTION

Antonio Muñoz Molina was born in 1956 in the Andalusian town of Úbeda and began his literary career with a series of articles published in the newspaper *Diario de Granada* in 1982 and 1983.¹ Ten years later he became one of Spain's most well-known living authors. In addition to his present popularity among non-academic readers, Muñoz Molina has also earned the esteem of literary critics and is now a member of Spain's *Real Academia de la Lengua*. He received the *Premio Ícaro* for his first novel, *Beatus ille* (1986), followed by both the *Premio de la Crítica* and the *Premio Nacional de Literatura* for *El invierno en Lisboa* (1987). Two years after publishing *Beltenebros* (1989), the author was again awarded the National Prize for Literature, as well as the coveted *Premio Planeta* for his fourth novel, *El jinete polaco* (1991).² Muñoz Molina has not only written novels and short stories, but is also an active journalist who has produced a steady stream of articles for Spain's major newspapers, including *ABC* and *El País*. He has published a history of Córdoba (*Córdoba de los omeyas*), a number of essays on literature,³ and a libretto for José García Román's one-act opera *El bosque de Diana*.⁴

Muñoz Molina's rapid rise to popularity is no doubt attributable to a combination of various factors, not least of which has been a concerted effort by Spanish publishers after Franco's death to promote the sale of works by young authors. However, aggressive marketing campaigns alone can not account for a work's appeal, and the commercial value of Muñoz Molina's fiction does not by any means imply its lack of literary merit or technical sophistication. Perhaps the author's primary achievement has been his understanding of—and identification with—his readers. Theories of reading have shown that a text may provoke a variety of responses from different audiences, an observation that Cervantes's Sansón Carrasco makes when describing the first part of *Don Quijote*: "es tan clara, que no hay cosa que dificultar en ella: los niños la manosean, los mozos la leen, los hombres la entienden y los viejos la celebran" (602). It is my belief that, like *Don Quijote*, Muñoz Molina's texts may be read for their obvious entertainment appeal, understood as self-reflexive commentaries on writing and reading, and celebrated as an important contribution to contemporary Spanish narrative of the post-transition era.

The novel of social realism

During the 1950s a number of novelists—identified by Santos Sanz Villanueva as "la generación del medio siglo"[5]—turned to documenting the decimating social and economic effects of the Spanish Civil War.[6] Although these authors were too young to have participated in the war as combatants, as children they were marked by their memories of the conflict and later by its ensuing consequences. Characteristic of their fiction was the use of realist techniques, also referred to as *neorrealismo* or *realismo social*, an approach which was encouraged by critics like José María Castellet, who "[d]ifundió y propugnó la idea de la necesidad de un arte arraigado en sus circunstancias históricas..." (*Historia* 37).[7] Literature thus served to both document and denounce in such novels as *Los bravos* (1954), *Duelo en el paraíso* (1955), *El Jarama* (1956), and *Central eléctrica* (1958).[8]

The experimentalist reaction

The publication of Luis Martín-Santos's *Tiempo de silencio* in 1962 signalled the beginning of a reaction against the social realist novel. There were four major reasons for this turn. First, there was an increasing awareness among social realist authors that their didactic intent had failed, for their works had neither succeeded in raising the consciousness of workers nor aided in toppling the Franco dictatorship. Second, the recuperation of the economy and large migrations from the countryside to urban centers presented authors with a dramatically changing society, the conditions of which could no longer be successfully documented with social realist techniques.[9] Third, the relaxation of censorship and the influence of the Latin American "boom" novels provided peninsular authors with exciting new possibilities for the formal renovation of narrative.[10] Finally, there was a feeling that social realism had not only been ineffective politically, but also deficient artistically, an opinion voiced by Juan Goytisolo in 1970:

> Si nuestra concepción estrecha del "realismo" cumplía, en apariencia, con nuestra responsabilidad moral y cívica, distaba mucho de responder a las exigencias culturales, artísticas y científicas del género y de la época....

> Para salir del atasco, había que luchar, en primer término, contra las formas artísticas envejecidas que nos aprisionaban e impedían seguir adelante. (*Disidencias* 164–65)

This rejection of realism provoked a turn to formal experimentation and self-reflexive strategies. Robert Spires writes that the neorealist novel of the 1950s "estriba en un lenguaje altamente referencial" and contrasts this to the "nueva novela" of the 1960s and 1970s, which supposes "un cambio de lenguaje referencial a uno auto-referencial" ("El nuevo lenguaje de la nueva novela" 6). Spires chooses two experimental novels, Luis Martín-Santos's *Tiempo de silencio* (1962) and Juan Goytisolo's *Juan sin tierra* (1975), to illustrate this turn to self-referentiality, and concludes by stating that the end of *Juan sin tierra*—written in Arabic—marked the death of the experimental novel: "Una libertad absoluta del lenguaje sólo puede terminar en silencio, o en la nada" (7). Yet it must be noted that experimental novels continued to be published after 1975—Julián Ríos's *Larva*[11] appeared in 1983—and conversely that not all narrative of the 1960s and '70s signified as radical an approach to language as that proposed by Goytisolo in *Juan sin tierra*.

The novel of the transition

There is general agreement among literary critics that the publication of Eduardo Mendoza's *La verdad sobre el caso Savolta* in 1975 marked another important turn in contemporary Spanish narrative: a reaction against the experimental novel's self-referentiality and formal complexity. The result was that while authors continued to incorporate certain structural aspects of the experimental novel, they began to exhibit a renewed interest in the simple pleasure of story-telling. This "Return to the Plot" (Eco 65) can be seen in the work of many authors of the 1970s and 1980s, including Eduardo Mendoza, Manuel Vázquez Montalbán, Juan Madrid, Rosa Montero and Luis Landero. During a symposium held in 1985, Santos Alonso, Andrés Amorós and Santos Sanz Villanueva agreed that

> one of the defining characteristics of the novel during the last decade has been the turning away from experimentalism and a return to realism and the pleasure of narrating stories. (Amell, *Literature* 14)

Five years later, opinions had not changed, and in answer to the question "¿Cuáles son, a su juicio, las lineas predominantes en la actual narrativa?" Andrés Amorós replied "Hoy, en general, se ha vuelto a las formas clásicas del relato: narraciones con argumento…" Carlos Galán Lorés identified "la recuperación del gusto por contar historias" and Juan Oleza "la pasión por contar cosas que tanto se menospreció en los 70 de los *novísimos*…" (Amorós et al. 9–11). Oleza added that

> [e]l experimentalismo y la metanarratividad han quedado incorporados a la novela de los 80, pero como una dimensión de fondo, no como su esquema vertebral. La novela actual…se sabe una ficción…pero la dirección dominante de su mirada ha regresado al relato, a la pasión de argumento. (Amorós et al. 11)

As will be seen, Muñoz Molina's work exemplifies both the experimental novel's metanarrative devices and that "passion for plot" which Oleza and others have identified as characteristic of the novel of the transition.

Muñoz Molina and "el desencanto"

In his public statements, Muñoz Molina has often stressed his support for the democratic-left ideals of the Second Republic, his abhorrence of Francoism, and his belief that the democratic transition after Franco's death was ultimately a failure. This last point is of great importance, for what many perceived as the inability of the Spanish Socialist Party (PSOE) to solve the country's social, political and economic problems was accompanied by a distinctive phenomenon called "el desencanto" (disillusionment), a term often used to characterize the period from 1975 to the present. José Carlos Mainer has identified the root of the "desencanto" as "the waning of the political and cultural leftist tradition, which used to be so sure of its historical right, of its power to interpret reality, and of its soul-winning vigor" ("Powers" 28). One of the reasons for what Mainer calls the "bankruptcy of the 'leftist tradition'" (29) is that the forces which had historically joined together in opposition to Franco suddenly lost their *raison d'être* after the dictator's death. It was not long after the electoral victory of the Socialists in 1982 that many Spaniards (including Muñoz Molina) who had been sympathetic to the values of the traditional left became disenchanted with the failure of the Socialists to fulfil their 1982 electoral promise embodied in their slogan "El cambio." Teresa Vilarós writes:

> A principios de los años setenta, la clase intelectual española estaba todavía necesariamente marcada y afectada por una utopía de transformación social revolucionaria y radical…. La utopía fue la droga de adicción de las generaciones que vivieron el franquismo. La muerte de Franco señala la retirada de la utopía…. El 75 representó el fin de la utopía, la constatación del desencanto… ("Los monos" 218, 221)[12]

In the chapters that follow, I will propose that Muñoz Molina's work is a post-transition manifestation of "el desencanto," not only thematically but also formally. Perhaps the most explicit thematic example is the short story "Nada del otro mundo," in which the narrator is seen pitying the former leftist militants whom he depicts as Spain's walking dead:

> los melancólicos peregrinos de izquierdas, los últimos mohicanos, los guardianes del fortín derribado, poseedores todavía de un carné del partido al que seguían llamando El Partido, aunque prácticamente hubiera dejado de existir... (*Nada del otro mundo* 39)

However, most of Muñoz Molina's texts do not thematize the question of "el desencanto" as explicitly as does "Nada del otro mundo," and it is the purpose of this study to go beyond the level of content in order to clarify how "el desencanto" also informs the author's approach to form and structure. In this way I hope to show that Muñoz Molina's approach to pre-existing genres—including the historical novel and the detective story—is the necessary result of a particular vision, one which reflects the collective experience of those in Spain who have lived to see their youthful utopian ideals defeated.

The Novel of Memory

Although there were early precedents, including Ana María Matute's *Primera memoria* (1960) and Juan Goytisolo's *Señas de identidad* (1966), what David Herzberger has called "novels of memory" ("Narrating the Past") became increasingly characteristic of the 1970s and 1980s. Fictional novels in which memory serves to recuperate and recount events of the Franco years include Juan Marsé's *Si te dicen que caí* (1973) and *La muchacha de las bragas de oro* (1978), Lourdes Ortíz's *Luz de la memoria* (1976), Jorge Semprún's *Autobiografía de Federico Sánchez* (1977), Carmen Martín Gaite's *Retahílas* (1974) and *El cuarto de atrás* (1978), Jose María Guelbenzu's *El río de la luna* (1981) and Luis Mateo Díez's *La fuente de la edad* (1986).

The novel of memory was a logical response to the traumatic social effects of Francoism, and a cathartic attempt by writers to come to terms with their past experiences under the dictatorship. Muñoz Molina continues this concern for recovering the past, and memory plays a key role in his fiction. "Mixing memory and desire" is the epigraph of his first novel, *Beatus ille*, which uses the Civil War and the ensuing years of Francoist repression as historical settings for a tale of intrigue. *Beltenebros* recreates the sordid atmosphere of Madrid during the dictatorship, and in *El dueño del secreto* an adult reminisces about his life as a young student in Madrid and his involvement in a conspiracy to overthrow the Franco regime. *El jinete polaco* is a generically eclectic work which combines autobiography, biography, and memoir in a homage to Proust's *A la recherche du temps perdu*.[13]

In Chapter 1 I discuss Muñoz Molina's conception of memory as a means of mediating reality and as a mental faculty that is often indistinguishable from imagination. Using examples from the author's articles, short stories and novels, I illustrate how his characters constantly confuse what they see with what they remember or simply imagine, and in the process obscure the distinction between reality and fiction. This results in undermining traditional notions of history, which as an objective record of the past becomes an increasingly unstable concept.

History and Metafiction

An important manifestation of the reaction against neorealism in Spain was the appearance of the "self-conscious" novel, defined by Robert Alter as "a novel that systematically flaunts its own condition of artifice" (*Partial Magic* x). In 1979 Gonzalo Sobejano referred to "[l]a reflexión autocrítica sobre el proceso de escribir (o leer)" as characteristic of many novels of the 1970s ("Ante la novela de los años setenta" 1), and in 1984 David Herzberger wrote that "metafiction is the most important mode of narrative in Spain today" ("Metafiction" 147). In 1989 Gonzalo Sobejano compiled a list of works ranging from Luis Goytisolo's *Recuento* (1973) to Juan José Millás's *El desorden de tu nombre* (1989) as exemplifying the Spanish "metanovela," or

> aquella novela que ante todo se refiere a sí misma como proceso de escritura, de lectura, de discurso oral, o como aplicación de una teoría exhibida en el propio texto. ("Novela y metanovela en España" 4)

It should be noted that whereas the Spanish novel of memory was for the most part a national response to the traumatic social effects of the Civil War, inspiration for the metafictional novel of the 1970s and 1980s came primarily from Latin American writers of the "boom." In 1986 Manuel Durán proposed that "[w]ith Borges, Cortázar, Rulfo, Fuentes, García Márquez, and Donoso active in Latin America, the Spanish novel was being pressured into a change of course" ("Fiction and Metafiction"

399), and when Carlos Fuentes was awarded the *Premio Cervantes* in 1988, Muñoz Molina wrote that the prize was

> una señal de gratitud por todo lo que la literatura española del último cuarto de siglo debe a algunos escritores hispanoamericanos.... Sin la llegada a España durante los años sesenta de la novela hispanoamericana no habría sido posible la pujanza de la novela española actual. ("Fábula de Fuentes")

There is no doubt that Muñoz Molina has been greatly influenced by Latin American writers like Borges, Onetti, Cortázar and García Márquez. However, his metafictional strategies are only the means to an end, which is to foreground the role of discourse in all narrative texts and in doing so call into question history's validity as an objective record of the past (Hutcheon, *Poetics* 105–23). In Chapter 2 I use *Beatus ille* and *Beltenebros* as examples of metafictions which, by challenging the historiographical assumptions of both Francoism and social realism, demythicize the heroic figures of the Republican Civil War poet and resistance member. This deconstructive project of questioning official versions of the past recalls Mainer's previously cited reference to "the waning of the political and cultural leftist tradition, which used to be so sure of its historical right, *of its power to interpret reality*" (Mainer, "Powers" 28; emphasis added). Epistemological doubt gives rise to disillusionment, and Muñoz Molina's characters are examples of "desencantados" who can no longer—to paraphrase an eighteenth-century document—hold any truths to be self-evident.

Reading and Intertextuality

The detective and crime novel experienced a spectacular rise in popularity among Spanish readers during the 1970s and 1980s, aided by the availability in Spanish translations of the works of Dashiell Hammet and Raymond Chandler.[14] By the time Muñoz Molina published his first novel, *Beatus ille*, Manuel Vázquez Montalbán, Andreu Martín, Jorge Martínez Reverte and Juan Madrid were already known for their *novelas negras*.[15] Paul Preston attributes the popularity of the *novela negra* to a need to denounce "the corruption and materialism of politics" in Spain,[16] and Muñoz Molina voiced a similar opinion in one of his newspaper articles: "No es casual que el éxito de los detectives americanos en España coincidiera casi exactamente con la declinación de los entusiasmos políticos" ("Los detectives"). If, as I propose, Muñoz Molina's vision is that of a "desencantado," it is not surprising that he has felt impelled to recreate the morally ambiguous and cynical worlds inhabited by Hammet and Chandler's detectives.

Muñoz Molina has never ceased to stress the importance of the reader and reading. In "Desocupado lector," he writes that "[e]l lector es el gran continente ignorado de la literatura" and that "la médula misma de la novela es el acto de leer." In Chapter 3 I use the reader-response theories of Wolfgang Iser to show how Muñoz Molina uses indeterminacy and hermeneutic gaps to engage his readers, and I follow with a discussion of the detective novel as an inherently metafictional genre that self-reflexively points to the acts of both writing and reading.[17] This prepares the analysis in Chapter 4 of how the author modifies his readers' generic expectations by parodying popular genres, including the nineteenth-century *folletín*, the crime novel, and its cinematic equivalent, *film noir*. My hypothesis proposes that none of the apparent playfulness with which Muñoz Molina parodies popular genres is gratuitous. On the contrary, the epistemological uncertainty and social pessimism that characterizes Spain's "desencantados" is reflected by the denial of complete narrative closure in *Beatus ille* and *El invierno en Lisboa*, and the ironic subversion of the "happy ending" in *Los misterios de Madrid*.

(Auto)biography and "self-conscious realism."

Novels of memory, as David Herzberger notes, "evoke past time through subjective remembering, most often through first-person narration" ("Narrating the Past" 35). Muñoz Molina consistently uses a first-person narrator, and in *El jinete polaco*, *Los misterios de Madrid*, *El dueño del secreto* and *Ardor guerrero* adopts autobiographical and biographical modes in order to problematize the distinction between fictional and factual narration. In Chapter 5 I discuss how in *El jinete polaco* and *El dueño del secreto* his approach to (auto)biography results in a "self-conscious realism," in which the reader is pulled in two opposite directions simultaneously, towards a metafictional and a realistic processing of the text. My conclusion is that Muñoz Molina's "self-conscious realism" allows him to create—as do Juan Marsé and Carmen Martín Gaite—metafictions which provide a realistic and Cervantine mirror of contemporary Spain and "el desencanto."

Notes

1. These articles appeared in *Diario de Granada* between May 1982 and June 1983. A number of them were later included in *El Robinson urbano*, along with "Todos los fuegos, el fuego," an article previously published in the now defunct magazine *Olvidos de Granada*.
2. Film versions have been made of both *El invierno* and *Beltenebros*. The former was directed by José Antonio Zorrilla and the latter by Pilar Miró. *Beltenebros* premiered in Madrid on December 13, 1991. For additional information on these films, see García-Moreno Barco.
3. *La realidad de la ficción* (Sevilla: Renacimiento, 1993) contains the texts of four lectures read at the *Fundación Juan March* in Madrid on January 22, 24, 29 and 31 of 1991. "La disciplina de la imaginación" is an essay that appears in *¿Por qué no es útil la literatura?* (Madrid: Ediciones Hiperión, 1993), which includes another essay by the poet Luis García Montero.
4. The libretto was published in the literary magazine *La Fábrica del Sur* (Separata del Núm. 3 [1990]: 5–22).
5. Sanz Villanueva uses the term "la generación del medio siglo" to refer to authors born between approximately 1924 and 1939, those who considered themselves "víctimas de la guerra, herederos morales de los vencidos y espectadores críticos de una degradada situación sociopolítica…" (*Historia* 34). Although some critics reject the term "generation" for its positivistic, deterministic, or ideological connotations, Sanz Villanueva adds that these authors share "rasgos biográficos y estéticos tan acentuados que forman un auténtico grupo, promoción, generación o como se quiera designar el fenómeno" (33–34).
6. One of the most tragic consequences of the Civil War was that a number of important writers—including Ramón Sender, Rafael Alberti, Francisco Ayala, and Max Aub—were forced into exile.
7. I use the term "realism" here not as a period concept, but rather as a general term that applies to all narrative in which the dominant function of language is "referential" rather than "poetic," following Roman Jakobson's definition of these functions in his "Linguistics and Poetics." For an excellent critique of period concepts of realism, see Jakobson's "On Realism in Art."

8 "Los temas [de la novela neorrealista], en su mayor parte, responden al deseo de presentar un testimonio cuasidocumental de la realidad social del país, con una intencionalidad crítica" (Sanz Villanueva, *Historia* 39).

9 "[P]ara expresar las nuevas circunstancias no es suficiente un mero testimonio" (Sanz Villanueva, *Historia* 158).

10 A similar process occurred at the beginning of the century when Rubén Darío and Vicente Huidobro helped to revolutionize Spanish poetry.

11 Not surprisingly, Juan Goytisolo praised *Larva* in a review. (See "La alquimia verbal de Julián Ríos" in Villanueva et al., pp. 368–70).

12 Vilarós's reference to 1975 as the beginning of the "desencanto" is somewhat misleading. In fact, revolutionary ideals did not die along with Franco, for the late 1970s were characterized by an explosion of leftist political activity, including a number of major demonstrations and strikes. Not until after the electoral victory of the Socialists in 1982 did the phenomenon became characteristic of many former anti-Francoists. At the same time, there were no doubt others who felt this disillusionment even before Franco died in 1975.

13 Although the events of *El invierno en Lisboa* occur in the 1980s, the narrator's reconstruction of Biralbo's life also depends on memory. See note 2 in the Conclusion.

14 See note 8 in Chapter 4.

15 For a history of the Spanish detective novel, see Hart.

16 [T]he cynical notion which lies at the heart of hard-boiled detective fiction…is a commonplace of Spanish, as of American, politics. For thirty five years before 1975, the manipulation of networks of corruption was one of General Franco's greatest skills…. The transition was a transaction negotiated in smoke-filled rooms. Accordingly, with the coming of democracy in Spain, there arrived a world identifiably afflicted with the corruption which is the subject of much American fiction. Spanish writers began to turn to a genre which…permits them an oblique, deeply moralistic, albeit ultimately impotent, comment on the corruption and materialism of politics… (Preston 10, 13).

17 Jorge Luis Borges, one of Muñoz Molina's professed models, was one of the first authors to exploit the self-reflexive nature of the detective genre in his well-known story "La muerte y la brújula."

Chapter One

Mixing Memory and Imagination

> inventar y recordar son tareas que se parecen mucho y de vez en cuando se confunden entre sí. (*La realidad de la ficción*)

The name of Muñoz Molina's fictional town, Mágina, was taken from Sierra Mágina, the toponym for a range of hills in Andalusia. It also evokes one of the author's primary themes: the i*magina*tion. Whether they be the tall tales of a boy's grandfather, the dreams of an adolescent trying to escape the stifling atmosphere of his home town, or the fictions that authors invent, for Muñoz Molina these are all manifestations of a basic and irrepressible human instinct, "nuestro hábito insomne de imaginar" ("El reino de las voces").

The question of the poetic imagination (or "fancy") was addressed by Hobbes in *Leviathan* (1651), and this treatise along with others like Locke's *Essay Concerning Human Understanding* (1690) laid the basis for subsequent eighteenth-century discussions that examined in considerable depth the creative and inventive processes of the mind. Theories of the poetic imagination are outlined in M. H. Abrams's *The Mirror and the Lamp*, in which the author concludes that, in the case of the romantics:

> [p]oetry...corresponds to objects which contain, or have been altered by, the feelings and *imagination* of the observer. The eye of the scientist passively receives, while the eye of the poet receives what it has itself supplemented or modified... (315; emphasis added)[1]

For romantic authors, imagination was a means of poetically transforming what they saw as a world increasingly devoid of aesthetic values. Baudelaire, whose rejection of bourgeois society was characteristic of the romantic movement in general, wrote:

> I find it useless and tiresome to portray things as they are, because nothing that exists satisfies me. Nature is ugly, and I prefer the monsters of my imagination to the triteness of actuality. (Qtd. in Hyslop 39)

There are echoes of Baudelaire in Muñoz Molina's references to "la antipatía de la realidad" ("Los libros y los trenes"), "las tediosas mujeres de la realidad" ("Correspondencia"), "el asedio inhóspito de la realidad" (*El Robinson urbano* 47) and "las crudas afrentas de la realidad" (*Diario del Nautilus* 19). It is therefore not surprising that in his texts imagination is treated—in Coleridge's words—as "the living power and prime agent of all human perception" (*Biographia Literaria* 167).

The ability of imagination to influence perception is the theme of Muñoz Molina's short story "La poseída" (*Nada del otro mundo*).[2] One morning, Marino—an office worker who has breakfast daily in the same café—notices a young girl whom he has never seen before. Entranced, he begins to observe her carefully and describes her bitten fingernails, the bags under her eyes, her glassy-eyed look and uncombed hair. He also notices that every morning she waits impatiently for an older man who comes to meet her at the café, and who passes her small packages. After only a few days, Marino concludes what must be happening: the girl is hopelessly in love with a married man who meets with her and gives her gifts. However, one morning the man does not appear at the café. When the girl enters a rest room but does not come out, Marino pushes open the door and finds her dead on the floor with a syringe lying beside her. Marino has imagined she was love-sick, when in reality she was a heroin addict and the man her "pusher."

"La poseída" is about a character who, like Cervantes's Don Quijote, Pérez Galdós's Isidora and Clarín's Bonifacio Reyes, lets his imagination blind him to reality. I use the word "blind" intentionally, for the irony of the story is that since Marino never speaks to the girl, he must deduce his version of the events exclusively from what he has seen. In "El personaje y su modelo," Muñoz Molina refers to the process of how, like Marino, we all create our personal versions of other people's lives, relying not only on our perceptions but also on our imagination:

> Usando datos de la percepción—que pueden estar distorsionados—construimos para los demás una vida como el novelista construye un personaje, y cuando más íntimamente creemos conocer es justo cuando más acabado es el trabajo de nuestra imaginación. (*La realidad de la ficción* 31)

On one level "La poseída" is simply another version of the perennial theme of reality versus illusion, yet it is also about the imagination as a narrative device. Hayden White posits that because "real events do not offer themselves as stories" ("The Value of Narrativity in the Representation of Reality" 4), raw perceptual data must be narrativized in order to be given any meaning. In his attempt to create a coherent explanation of the girl's behavior, Marino creates his personal narrative of love-sickness, demonstrating what White calls "a desire to have real events display the coherence, integrity, fullness, and closure of an image of life that is and *can only be imaginary*" ("The Value" 24; emphasis added). Although Marino's narrative explanation is plausible enough, it is only a fiction:

> somos una mezcla inquietante de realidad y ficción, de verdad y mentira, un precipitado de signos cuya fisonomía y carácter dependen no de su propia identidad, sino del modo en que los elabora nuestra mirada y nuestra imaginación. (*La realidad de la ficción* 32-3)

Marino's activity as a *voyeur* and as an imaginative forger of narratives has its antecedent in Muñoz Molina's "Urban Robinson." Robinson is the author's alter ego:

> Para quien frecuenta, a solas, las estaciones y los aeropuertos, cada una de las fugaces vidas ajenas que se cruzan con la suya contiene las posibilidad de una historia… ("Teoría del adiós")

The Urban Robinson is an observer of the city, a "mirón" (*El Robinson urbano* 14) who "mil ojos abiertos quisiera tener para percibir de un solo golpe todas las cosas que la ciudad le ofrece" (15). He does more than simply observe, however, and also uses his imagination to narrativize. Like Marino, Robinson "[r]econoce caras que ha visto en el autobús, [y] les asigna una historia" (*El Robinson urbano* 15).

"La colina de los sacrificios" (*Nada del otro mundo*) is, like "La poseída," an account of how a subject's imagination leads him to an erroneous interpretation of events. In this story, a police inspector is in possession of the fractured skull of a woman who has been killed with an axe. As the inspector interviews the suspected murderer, he imaginatively reconstructs the events of the crime by first envisioning the gasoline station where the suspect had worked: "imaginaba un paisaje despojado y remoto…" (153). He then attempts to picture the suspect, "queriendo *imaginar* cuál habría sido su aspecto quince años atrás…. Lo *imaginó* silencioso e inhábil…" (153); "El inspector lo *imaginó* hundido en los cojines del sofá..." (157; emphases added). Having created his own version of the murder and confident that the suspect is guilty, the inspector is ordered to the forensic surgeon's office. There he learns from an archaeologist that the skull is over fifteen hundred years old and that the scene of the murder was also an ancient sacrificial site. The inspector has failed to grasp the truth because—like Marino in "La poseída"—he has become the victim of his own narrative imagination.

In "El hombre sombra," the protagonist, Santiago Pardo, is in bed one night when his telephone rings. Although it is two o'clock in the morning, he is lonely and anxious to speak with somebody, so he picks up the receiver only to hear a woman, Nélida, ask for Mario. As Santiago is about to hang up, he realizes that due to a telephone-wire malfunction he is able to overhear half of the conversation—half, because of the two voices he can hear only Nélida's. Santiago realizes that Nélida can not hear him, so when the same phenomenon occurs two nights later he decides to listen until she hangs up, imagining that she is speaking to him instead of to Mario:

> como un mirón tras una cerradura, oía la voz muy pronto reconocida y deseada imaginando que era a él a quien le hablaba para recordarle los pormenores de una caricia o de una cita clandestina. (*Nada del otro mundo* 77)

Lonely and frustrated, Santiago longs for an intimate relationship with a woman and continues to eavesdrop on Nélida's telephone conversations, fantasizing about this woman whose voice "le encendía el deseo de su cuerpo invisible" (77). Because he cannot see her, he begins to imagine her physical appearance by combining fragments of information that he overhears with details from his own imagination:

> Veía, sí, sus ojos, el pelo suelto y largo, acaso su boca y su sonrisa, una falda amarilla y una blusa blanca que ella dijo una vez que acababa de comprarse, unos zapatos azules, cierto perfume cuyo nombre no alcanzó a escuchar. (78)

Although Santiago can not hear the man's voice, he also imagines what Mario must be like:

> Se complacía en adivinarlo insolente y turbio, minuciosamente vulgar, con anchas corbatas de colores, con pulseras de plata en las muñecas velludas. (77–8)

Santiago has no difficulty in conjuring up these images of Nélida and Mario, because he is by nature prone to fantasy:

> le acabó suciediendo, como ya era su costumbre, que se imaginaba vivir dentro de una película de intriga, y que un espía o perseguidor del enemigo lo estaba siguiendo por la ciudad. (75)

Santiago decides to see Nélida one day where she has arranged to meet Mario. As he approaches the spot, he sees a woman waiting whom he is sure must be Nélida:

> No era alta, desde lejos, pero sí rubia y altiva y a la vez dócil a la desdicha.... La falda amarilla, sí, los ojos ocultos tras unas gafas de sol, la nariz y la boca que al principio lo desconcertaron porque eran exactamente la parte de Nélida que él no había sabido imaginar. (79–80)

Lacking the nerve to talk to her, he only asks her to light his cigarette, and the story ends as he hurries back to his room feeling cowardly and ashamed.

Imagination is the primary motif of "El hombre sombra," for like many others of Muñoz Molina's characters, including Marino and the inspector, Santiago invents his own narrative version of events—in this case Nélida's doomed relationship with Mario. However, given that Santiago ultimately fails to communicate with Nélida, his imagination only serves to ironically contrast his fantasy of replacing Mario as Nélida's lover with the reality of his own timidity and emotional frustration. Although perhaps not one of Muñoz Molina's best short stories, "El hombre sombra" does underscore the author's conception of the imagination as a faculty that duplicates the effects of sensual impressions: Santiago's imaginary portrait of Nélida is so vivid that he is described as "seeing" her as he listens to her voice on the telephone ("podía verla con absoluta claridad..." [76]; "Veía, sí, sus ojos..." [78]).

Like Marino and Santiago, many of Muñoz Molina's characters resort to their imagination in order to escape their feelings of solitude and alienation produced by urban life: "para mí el sentimiento de Robinson es el sentimiento de soledad en medio de una ciudad..." (Martín Gil 24). Muñoz Molina has often praised the Uruguayan Juan Carlos Onetti,[3] and one reason that he has chosen this author as a literary model is that Onetti's characters are also typical products of urban alienation who use fantasy as a psychological release. According to Djelal Kadir:

> Onetti's characters respond in the same way that their creator has chosen to face this futile human condition, by turning to the sphere of fantasy, the dream world, the realm of creative imagination. (42)

Similarly, Hugo Verani writes of Onetti's characters:

> Los sueños y los ensueños son variaciones del mismo tema y su función es ofrecer una compensación, en el plano de lo imaginario, a la crisis afectiva de los protagonistas (34).[4]

As well as providing his lonely and alienated adult characters an escape from "al asedio inhóspito de la realidad," the imagination is for Muñoz Molina also characteristic of infants and adolescents. In *Beatus ille*, the child Minaya envisions his father as a heroic comic-book character—"imaginando que su verdadero padre...era...el Coyote o el Capitán Trueno o el Guerrero del Antifaz" (10)—and in *El jinete polaco*, the young Manuel sees rats and snakes in the countryside, "que la imaginación convertía, sobre todo de noche, en caimanes y tigres, en serpientes pitón, en juancaballos voraces" (25). Like many adolescents raised in small rural towns, Manuel longs to escape Mágina and turns to a fantasy world where he imagines himself in a number of different roles:

> Quería cambiar a mi antojo de nombre, de ciudad, de país y de idioma, y mientras caminaba solo por las calles de Mágina...estaba inventándome de manera incesante pasados y porvenires, y había días y semanas enteras que dedicaba a la invención detallada de una sola vida, en París, por ejemplo, con diecinueve años...escribiendo piezas de teatro del absurdo en una buhardilla, o en San Francisco, de batería de rock... (*El jinete polaco* 256)

Manuel's adolescent fantasies are similar to those of the author's other adult characters, and the title of the anthology *Las otras vidas* underscores the incessant activity of those who—like Onetti's characters—imagine themselves taking on other identities.

In "Arte nuevo de escribir novelas" Muñoz Molina states that "toda novela perdurable es una cristalización de la memoria..." (14). Like the imagination, memory is another fundamental motif in almost all of Muñoz Molina's texts, for his characters are depicted as continually remembering (and forgetting) a personal or collective past. In *Beatus ille*, the story of a Civil War poet is slowly revealed through the recollections of all the characters who have known him. In *El invierno en Lisboa*, the story of Santiago Biralbo is contingent both on the latter's own memory of the past and on that of the narrator. The agent Darman in *Beltenebros* is haunted by memories of one of his victims, Walter. *El jinete polaco* is a contemporary version of Proust's *A la recherche du temps perdu*, and *El dueño del secreto* is a fictive memoir of a narrator who reminisces about his participation in a political conspiracy in 1974.

Because Muñoz Molina is a creative writer and not an academic philosopher, he never explicitly defines memory. However, in his article "Objetos encontrados" he refers to the futility of what he calls "conscious memory:" "El recuerdo consciente es casi siempre un ejercicio de amnesia, porque la memoria, aislada de las sensaciones, se obstina en el vacío y segrega mentiras." The author's term "recuerdo consciente" recalls Proust's conception of "mémoire volontaire." Before his experience with the tea and the *madeleine*, Marcel can only remember Combray as two floors joined by a staircase at seven o'clock:

> A vrai dire, j'aurais pu répondre à qui m'eût interrogé que Combray comprenait encore autre chose et existait à d'autres heures. Mais comme ce que je m'en serais rappelé m'eût été fourni seulement par *la mémoire volontaire, la mémoire de l'intelligence, et comme les renseignements qu'elle donne sur le passé ne conservent rien de lui*, je n'aurais jamais eu envie de songer à ce reste de Combray.... Il en est ainsi de notre passé. C'est peine perdue que nous cherchions à l'évoquer, *tous les efforts de notre intelligence sont inutiles*. (44; emphases added).

In a personal interview, Muñoz Molina spoke of his conscious debt to the French author:

> Proust, lo que hace es la reivindicación de la memoria inconsciente, y la memoria inconsciente hecha a través de la sensación.... La lección de Proust para mí es que la memoria consciente miente. La memoria consciente y la inteligencia consciente están llenas de mentiras, y que únicamente la memoria inconsciente o la atención como sesgada, la atención que va detrás de lo que parecen ser las cosas, es lo que te explica el tiempo. (Rich 1992)

A Proustian conception of memory is evident throughout *El jinete polaco*, and at one point Manuel says "es mentira la certidumbre del recuerdo consciente" (275). While conscious memory fails him, Manuel also has experiences of "mémoire involontaire" similar to Marcel's:

> Y es ahora, mientras le hablo a Nadia, mientras las palabras vienen a mis labios tan *involuntariamente* y tan sin tregua ni orden como las imágenes de un sueño, cuando *surge ante mí un recuerdo intacto y perdido*... (189; emphases added)

Just as the imagination may deceive—as in the case of Marino in "La poseída" and the inspector in "La colina de los sacrificios"—so is "conscious memory" capable of distorting, modifying, or transforming one's perception of past events. Muñoz Molina repeatedly underscores this instability of memory in both his essays and his fiction, referring to "la inexactitud de la memoria" ("La mano de nieve"), "los hábitos mentirosos de la memoria" ("Las máquinas del tiempo"), "la arbitraria lógica de los recuerdos" (*Diario del Nautilus* 54), "la memoria inútil" (*Beltenebros* 92) and "la memoria impotente" (*El jinete polaco* 30).

Because both imagination and memory mediate perception, in Muñoz Molina's texts the two faculties are often associated and at times even identified with each other. In *La realidad de la ficción* he writes, "inventar y recordar son tareas que se parecen mucho y de vez en cuando se confunden entre sí. La memoria está inventando de manera incesante nuestro pasado... (29–30). This (con)fusion of memory and imagination is a recurring motif in the author's texts. In *Beatus ille*, the poet Solana speaks of "la historia que yo imagino y recuerdo..." (211), and Minaya "imaginaba aquella escena como un recuerdo propio..." (201). In *El invierno en Lisboa*, Santiago wanders through Lisbon "recorriendo con el dedo índice los mapamundis de su imaginación y su memoria..." (125), while in *Beltenebros* Darman says "Recordé mi casa como si la viese desde fuera.... Imaginaba el interior..." (34). According to Manuel in *El jinete polaco*, "lo que yo supongo invención en realidad es una forma invulnerada de memoria..." (194), and he later confesses that "se me confunden los hilos de la imaginación y la memoria..." (508).

The greater part of Muñoz Molina's fiction is informed by the belief that *all* perception is subjective, contingent, and mediated by memory and imagination. The author writes in "La manera de vivir:"

> Miro para saber, pero la mirada miente y las apariencias engañan, *tal vez con más eficacia que la imaginación y el recuerdo*, con más exactitud, pero sigo mirando porque no conozco otro remedio contra la mentira... (emphasis added)

Here, Muñoz Molina associates physical perception ("la mirada") with mental constructions ("la imaginación y el recuerdo"), suggesting an affinity between the two. Thus, when his characters remember or imagine a scene, they often describe it as if it were the direct product of sensual experience. In the first section of *El jinete polaco*, the narrator forms a mental image of Mágina while in Nadia's New York apartment:

> *Veo* encenderse una a una las luces en los miradores de Mágina.... *No cuenta la memoria sino la mirada*, *veo* en la penumbra fría ese resplandor que se hace

más vivo a medida que la oscuridad va ganando la calle, *huelo* a humo y a frío... (19)

Oigo...la voz de mi abuelo Manuel... (28; emphases added)

By deliberately blurring the boundaries between memory, imagination and sensual perception, Muñoz Molina makes "reality" a relative term, the meaning of which is entirely contingent on the subject's perception as mediated by imagination and memory.

The interdependence of memory and imagination was noted by T. S. Eliot in his essay "Wordsworth and Coleridge," in which he gives the following example:

> There might be the experience of a child of ten, a small boy peering through sea-water in a rock-pool, and finding a sea-anemone for the first time: the simple experience...might lie dormant in his mind for twenty years, and re-appear transformed in some verse-context charged with great imaginative pressure. *There is so much memory in imagination...*" ("Wordsworth" 79; emphasis added)

Eliot assumes that the content of memory can subsequently be transformed by the imagination. However, for Muñoz Molina the reverse process can also occur, when imagination may be conditioned by memory. As the narrator says of Nadia in *El jinete polaco*, "Su imaginación se había educado en los recuerdos españoles de su padre..." (213). Characters are frequently depicted perceiving events through the filter of their memories, including fictional scenes from films they have seen. For Manuel's mother, "subir a la plaza del General Orduña y a la calle Nueva sería como visitar otro mundo más parecido al cine que a la realidad..." (141), and when she is about to give birth, the wind and the rain outside her home strike "con una furia que le hacía acordarse de las tormentas que provocaban naufragios en el cine..." (166–67). A fireplace reminds the young Manuel of "las erupciones de volcanes que había visto en el cine" (174), and when Nadia meets with "El Praxis" in a bar,

> le pareció un lugar opresivo, pero también caliente y abrigado, casi novelesco, con aquellas caras sombrías que la miraban fijamente y que le hicieron acordarse de los guerrilleros de boina calada, cejas peludas y piel cobriza y aceitosa que le ayudaban a Gary Cooper en *Por quién doblan las campanas*. (364)

Similarly, when a character hears of a real person or place s/he has not seen, the comparison is often to a fiction. When Manuel's grandfather writes to his wife from a concentration camp, the young Manuel imagines it to be "como los campos de concentración de las películas" (107), and when Don Mercurio describes to Ramiro the night he was kidnapped, in Ramiro's imagination "fue cobrando un torvo romanticismo de litografía y de folletín…" (128).

In "Juego de las conmemoraciones" (*El Robinson urbano*), the author self-consciously underscores his vision of the city as intertextually mediated by memory and the literary imagination:

> Varios siglos de literatura y algunas décadas de folletos en papel couché para el turismo favorecen un espejismo que perdura sobre la mediocre realidad, que avanza sobre ella y a veces llega a suplantarla, ocupando territorios enteros, calles numeradas por la imaginación y plazas que parecen concebidas para justificar una cita, una metáfora. Hay horas en que la noche se pone íntima como una pequeña plaza,[5] y días enteros en que el Paseo de los Tristes no es un lugar de Granada, sino un paisaje de la literatura…. Sobre el plano visible de la ciudad se impone una segunda ciudad imaginaria, un tapiz en cuyo delicado dibujo se enlazan los pormenores de la fascinación y la memoria… (25)

If for Muñoz Molina imagination and memory are basic human faculties which are constantly mediating perception, "objective" observation is impossible, for what is seen is always mentally transformed by the observer. In his introduction to Ricardo Martín's book of photographs, *Sostener la Mirada. Imágenes de la Alpujarra*, Muñoz Molina writes:

> La literatura da cuenta del mundo inventándolo: igual hace la fotografía, es decir, la mirada. No hay un mundo exterior que los ojos perciban cuyas imágenes queden impresionadas en la corteza cerebral o en el breve rectángulo de la película. La inteligencia, la astucia, el adiestramiento de quien mira construyen el mundo igual que lo construía el pintor del siglo XV mediante la perspectiva. La mirada, desde luego, pareciendo tan natural, es histórica… (n. pag.)

By referring to the observer's "construction" of the world, Muñoz Molina underscores the role of the perceiving subject, a question of fundamental import in all of his narrative. Given the determining role of the subject in perceiving reality through the mediating filters of memory and imagination, it is not surprising that Muñoz Molina favors the use of a first-person narrator, a deliberate attempt to focus on the problem of subjective narration.

First- and Third-Person Narration

The concept of voice is essential to any discussion of narrative: "la voz del narrador constituye la única realidad del relato" (Tacca 69). For Muñoz Molina, voice is not simply a theoretical term but a physical reality, and orality is consequently an important aspect of his narrative worlds, in which characters are depicted speaking and listening to each other more often than they are writing or reading. Telephones, radios, and tape-recorders are constantly employed and emphasize the author's preoccupation with the spoken word. In "El hombre sombra," Santiago listens to Nélida over the telephone, while in *El jinete polaco* Manuel leaves messages on Nadia's answering machine and learns of his grandmother's death by telephone. In *Beatus ille*, Manuel and Medina listen to Radio Pirenaica, and in *El jinete polaco*—the first part of which is entitled "El reino de las voces"—radio *folletines* are a key element in the plot. *Los misterios de Madrid* is a story which before being written has been recorded by Lorencito Quesada, who never goes anywhere without his portable cassette-player, and Quesada reappears in the story "El cuarto del fantasma" (*Las otras vidas*), in which he also uses a cassette to record don Palmiro's story.

In "Noticia de una tentativa" Muñoz Molina mentions "una triple fascinación," which includes "la de los relatos orales," and in *La realidad de la ficción* he notes:

> una de las imágenes más vividas de mi niñez no procede de un recuerdo visual, sino de la voz profunda de mi abuelo materno contándome la historia de una mujer a la que enterraron viva… (47)

Born in a rural and predominantly oral society,[6] from an early age Muñoz Molina fell under the spell of the spoken word, and on more than one occasion has expressed his desire to achieve the seductive power of oral narration through writing: "[el] deseo de que las palabras que uno mismo escribe adquieran en el alma y en la imaginación de quien las lea el sonido cálido e indudable de una voz" ("El reino de las voces"). As Solana declares in *Beatus ille*: "Basta mi conciencia y la soledad y las palabras que pronuncio en voz baja para guiarla…. Ya no es preciso escribir para adivinar o inventar las cosas" (8).

Muñoz Molina's treatment of the narrating subject as one whose perception is continually mediated by imagination and memory may be seen as a challenge to the nineteenth-century realist ideal of the narrator as an impassive and objective observer of a pre-existing reality. For Benito Pérez

Galdós, the novel should be an "espejo fiel de la sociedad en que vivimos" ("Observaciones" 163), and in the same article Galdós deplores the popularity of the *folletín* in which "más nos agrada imaginar que observar" (163). Authors like Galdós and Clarín often use characters who exemplify the nefarious effects of subjective idealization: in Galdós's *La deseheredada* and Clarín's *La Regenta*, Isidora and Ana are characters who are victims of their own imaginative fantasies. To allow the reader to distinguish between the characters' imaginative illusions and the harsh reality of their social environment, such realist authors tend to utilize a narrator both perceptually and cognitively superior to the characters portrayed, one who has traditionally been referred to as "omniscient." This term, however, can be misleading because it does not necessarily entail the use of a third-person voice, and Galdós often relies on a homodiegetic narrator[7] to reinforce verisimilitude. This use of a first-person narrator presents a particular problem for the realist project: an eye-witness may be a guarantor of verisimilitude,[8] but s/he does not always have access to information nor is always able to relay it successfully. Human perception, judgement and memory are notoriously limited, and first-person narration is always potentially deceptive or unreliable.[9] Galdós and others found an ingenious way of circumventing this problem and maintaining not only verisimilitude but also narratorial reliability and omniscience: the use of a grammatically chameleonic narrator who alternates between first and third person. A canonical example is Galdós's *Fortunata y Jacinta*, in which a first-person narrator acts as a "historian," narrating what he has seen and what he has been told by reliable sources.[10] Although his status as a character in the story should theoretically limit his access to information, these limitations are overcome when the use of first-person pronouns and verbs are intermittently dropped and the narrator—assuming the function of an omniscient third-person voice—is able to account for the thoughts and dreams of the other characters. Readers have learned to naturalize this protean narrator, and the resulting convention has proven to be an effective strategy in realistic fiction from the nineteenth century to the present day.[11] I will now discuss how Muñoz Molina utilizes this convention while deliberately and self-reflexively problematizing it.

The significance of first- and third-person voice is examined by Emile Benveniste, who makes a distinction between history and discourse as two distinct verbal systems ("The Correlations of Tense in the French Verb"). Besides requiring specific past tenses (207), historical narration must be in the third person in order to eliminate all traces of the enunciating subject (deictics). In contrast, in discourse all tenses but the aorist may be used and "the relationship of person is everywhere present" (209). This distinction has certain weaknesses because it is extremely difficult to remove all traces of an enunciator, and Jonathan Culler notes that "[h]owever much a text strives to be pure story in Benveniste's terms, it will still contain features that characterize a particular narrative stance" (*Structuralist* 198–99). Another problem is that Benveniste rejects what he considers to be the false dichotomy of written history versus spoken discourse, given that "discourse is written as well as spoken" ("The Correlations" 209), but he fails to mention the logical corollary: history is spoken as well as written. Since no enunciation can be conceived of without an enunciator, Susan Lanser observes that "there is technically no such entity as a third-person narrator because there is no enunciation without a speaking subject" (176).

The impossibility of overlooking the mediating presence of an enunciating subject in so-called "third-person narration" is a key to understanding Muñoz Molina's fiction. "La poseída" and "La colina de los sacrificios" are ostensibly narrated by an objective and omniscient third-person voice, but a close reading reveals that neither story eliminates the point of view of the protagonist, a phenomenon addressed by Roland Barthes in his essay "An Introduction to the Structural Analysis of Narrative." Barthes points out that a third-person narrator may only be a subterfuge for what is in reality a "personal" system of narration, which for Benveniste pertains to the plane of discourse: "Some narratives…can very well be written in the third person, although their real stance is the first person" (Barthes, "Introduction" 262). Since the events in "La poseída" and "La colina de los sacrificios" are for the most part focalized[12] through their respective protagonists, one need only do as Barthes suggests—change all third-person pronouns to the first person—to confirm the effect of homodiegetic narration:

> Apenas cruzaba la puerta, el camarero ya se apresuraba a buscar el periódico del día para ofercérse[me]lo y ponía en la cafetera un tazón de desayuno, saludándlo[me] con una sonrisa de hospitalidad, casi de dulzura. Marino [Yo] llevaba meses apreciendo a la misma hora en el bar y marchándose[me] justo veinte minutos más tarde… ("La poseída" 93)

> Creyó [creí] haber oído que alguien repetía su [mi] nombre por un altavoz. Se acordó [Me acordé] del forense…y sintió [sentí] un acceso de ira… ("La colina de los sacrificios" 155)

This fusion of personal and impersonal modes of narration is characteristic of Muñoz Molina's fiction, and is a topic addressed in his essay "La voz y el estilo" (*La realidad de la ficción*). Examining the relative benefits of first- and third-person narration, he first notes the persuasive power of an omniscient voice:

> [Un narrador en tercera] puede contarnos lo que quiera a condición de que no varíe el tono, puede, a su gusto, callar o explicar, porque es él quien lo sabe todo y nosotros quienes miramos fascinados sus labios. (59)

In spite of this eulogy to the traditionally seductive effect of an omniscient narrator, Muñoz Molina also admits that his attempts to write in the third person have inevitably resulted in having to resort to a homodiegetic narrator:

> [Las historias] he comenzado siempre en tercera persona, y siempre, metódicamente, han fracasado al cabo de unos pocos capítulos, y he tenido que volver al principio para encarnarlas en una voz que participara de los hechos... (*La realidad de la ficción* 63)[13]

This was the case in *El invierno en Lisboa*, which he began to write in the third person, only to revert to a first-person narrator:

> Para mí, el narrador es quizá el elemento más brillante.... El narrador *hace de ojo, de testigo, testigo parcial*. Conseguir ese efecto fue para mí un reto, un 'tour de force.' (Solana VII; emphasis added)

Through his reconstruction of Santiago Biralbo's story, the anonymous narrator of *El invierno en Lisboa* serves to emphasize the importance of observation, imagination and memory. He is first introduced as an eyewitness observer: "Habían pasado casi dos años desde la última vez que vi a Santiago Biralbo" (9); "vi el perfil de Biralbo" (9); "lo estuve observando" (10); "Observé" (10). However, the reader soon learns that Biralbo's ill-fated adventure began years before, and that the narrator has personally witnessed only a fraction of the story's key events. Muñoz Molina's term "testigo parcial" could not be more appropriate, for the narrator is "partial" in two ways: he has seen very little of what has actually occurred, and he is also partial *to* Santiago in the sense of being biased or prejudiced in his favor. In fact, the two friends are strikingly alike. Both are solitary, both are regular drinkers and have similar tastes in alcohol ("la similitud de preferencias alcohólicas" [11]; "íbamos a los mismos bares" [53]), and both are attracted sexually to Mónica, the waitress. The identification between the two men is such that it almost causes them to switch roles: as Biralbo begins to tell his story to the narrator, the latter says "Temía que si continuaba iba a empezar a hablarle de mi vida a Biralbo" (14). They are able to read each other's minds, "sabiendo cada uno lo que el otro pensaba" (30), and the narrator even states at one point that "era a Biralbo y no a mí a quien debía ocurrírsele ese pensamiento" (36).

The quasi-symbiotic relationship between the narrator and Biralbo sets the stage for the former to imaginatively recreate those parts of Biralbo's story he has never witnessed. Although he is able to piece together parts of the musician's life with the aid of photographs, newspaper clippings and what he has seen, remembered, or been told by Biralbo and others, portions of the story are evidently pure conjecture. For example, after Biralbo tells him that Lucrecia and Malcolm had left San Sebastián on a ship, the narrator begins to imagine the scene. Since neither he nor Biralbo were present to observe the events, he uses conditional verbs and expressions of doubt:

> A uno de ellos [los veleros] subieron Malcolm y Lucrecia, temiendo *acaso* perder el equilibrio mientras llevaban sus maletas.... Mientras el barco se adentraba en la oscuridad *oirían* con alivio el lento estrépito del motor en el agua. *Debieron de* volverse para mirar desde lejos el faro de la isla.... *Supongo que* a esa misma hora Biralbo bebía crudo bourbon.... *Me pregunté si* Lucrecia había acertado a distinguir en la lejanía las luces del Lady Bird... (41; emphases added)

Muñoz Molina has often stressed his admiration for William Faulkner,[14] and there is a striking parallel between this passage and Chapter 4 of *Absalom, Absalom!* In Faulkner's novel, no one witnesses the dispute between Henry Sutpen and Charles Bon, and consequently the characters spend hours trying to reconstruct events, often through pure speculation. It is likely that Muñoz Molina used *Absalom, Absalom!* as an intertext, for Compson uses the same expressions of conditionality and doubt as the narrator of *El invierno en Lisboa*: "*Perhaps* that is what went on" (96); "He *had probably* not paid enough attention" (98); "He *must have known*" (106). When the narrator of *El invierno en Lisboa* stresses the speculative component of his narrative by saying "Puedo imaginar" (46), he is echoing Compson, who repeats "I can imagine" (108); "Yes, I can imagine" (109).

In addition to relying on his imagination, the narrator of *El invierno en Lisboa* also uses his recollection of past events to piece together Biralbo's story. From the opening sentence, references to his own memory saturate the text: "Habían pasado casi dos años desde la última vez que vi a Santiago Biralbo…" (9); "Recordé que en San Sebastián…" (11); "Me acordaba únicamente de la ciudad…" (12); "me parecía en el recuerdo…" (12); "Entonces me acordé…" (12); "me acordé de Lucrecia…" (13), etc. However, his memory often fails him ("había olvidado todo lo que Biralbo me contó…" [12]), and this is underscored several times as he mentions "una canción cuyo título no supe recordar" (9), "una foto en la que Lucrecia no se parece nada a mis recuerdos" (46) and "un recuerdo inexacto de aquella noche" (85). Biralbo's memory, too, is subject to time's assault: "quiso recordar…y no pudo lograrlo" (38); "El no recordaba que comimos juntos aquel día" (73); "no acertaba a distinguir entre el desconocimiento y el recuerdo" (124). Both imagination and memory serve to highlight the limitations of an eye-witness narrator, making what Scholes and Kellogg say of Proust equally applicable to Muñoz Molina:

> [His] entire esthetic…continually mentions the limitations of the empirical and asserts the extraordinary power of those insubstantial essences, memory and imagination. (*The Nature of Narrative* 260–1)

While Muñoz Molina believes that an individual's memory and imagination mediate his/her perception of reality, he deliberately uses third-person narration as a device to disguise or mitigate the presence of a subjective narrator. In the two short stories mentioned, we have seen how he achieves the effect of first-person narration by focalization through the protagonist. A similar process occurs in *El invierno en Lisboa*, for although it is narrated by a first-person voice, the narrator often drops his "I" to relate extensive passages that grammatically qualify as third-person narration. A close reading reveals that these passages are in fact focalized through Biralbo:

> [Yo] *Notaba* la serenidad letal de quien sabe que se está ahogando y se volvía [me volvía] para mirar el rótulo del *Burma*.… [Yo] *Percibía* cada instante como un minuto larguísimo y [yo] *miraba* los rostros… (142; emphases added)

The above passage and others like it give the impression of the narrator experiencing events directly through Biralbo, just as the narrator "sees" through the eyes of Marino in "La poseída" and the inspector in "La colina de los sacrificios." However, there is a fundamental difference between these two short stories and *El invierno en Lisboa*. Whereas in the short stories an omniscient third-person narrator is used to focalize through the protagonist, in *El invierno en Lisboa* it is a first-person limited narrator who focalizes through Biralbo. Thus, the narration of Biralbo's actions and thoughts is inevitably contingent on both Biralbos's *and* the narrator's imagination and memory. The narrator may attempt to "disappear" by dropping references to his "I," but the reader is continually reminded that the account of Biralbo's adventures is in fact the product of two limited narrators' imaginative fantasies and subjective memories. When the narrator insists that he "sees" rather than "imagines" events, he is self-consciously and ironically pointing out that the opposite is really the case. Although he was never present to see Biralbo's meeting with Lucrecia in the bar La Gaviota, the narrator insists: "*No imagino* estas cosas, no busco sus pormenores en las palabras que me ha dicho Biralbo. *Las veo* como desde muy lejos…" (67–68; emphases added).

The narrator of *El invierno en Lisboa* is not the only character who blurs the distinction between imagination ("No imagino") and observation ("las veo"). Like the narrator, Biralbo is also continually creating his own imaginative version of events, although in his case it has had a specifically pernicious effect. The author has attributed Biralbo's failure to establish a relationship with Lucrecia to romantic idealization, stating:

> su relación con la chica es una relación nula, porque sólo saben encontrarse en lo imaginario; no saben encontrarse en lo real. Y esto es una maldición para ellos. (Ribas 52)

This is evident as Biralbo and Lucrecia talk together one evening in the Lady Bird:

> Con un tranquilo ademán [Lucrecia] posó su mano en el teclado y le pidió que la mirara.
> —No me has mirado aún—dijo—. Todavía no has querido mirarme.
> —No he hecho otra cosa desde que me llamaste. Antes de verte ya te estaba imaginando.
> —No quiero que me imagines…. Quiero que me veas. (81)

Employing a third-person voice to disguise the presence of the narrator is one of the author's characteristic strategies and a key element in *Beatus ille*, *El invierno en Lisboa*, *El jinete polaco* and *Los misterios de Madrid*. *El jinete polaco* begins in the third person: "Sin que se dieran cuenta se les hizo de noche…" (9). However, this third-person voice alternates with that of Manuel, who soon enters as a first-person narrator: "ha anochecido sin que nos diéramos cuenta" (31). As in *El invierno en Lisboa*, extensive passages of *El jinete polaco* written in the third person are focalized through Manuel, and could easily be rewritten in the first person:

> Se incorporó [Me incorporé] para buscar un cigarillo en la mesa de noche y sólo entonces se dio cuenta [me di cuenta] de lo tarde que era al ver la hora en el despertador, y calculó [calculé] instintivamente la hora que sería en Mágina.... Miró [miré] el teléfono y se acordó [me acordé]... (12–13)

As well as making *El jinete polaco* generically ambiguous—one might call it either a fictional autobiography or biography—this technique again underscores that impersonal narration is only an illusion, for it often masks the presence of a subjective narrator.

Los misterios de Madrid provides a minor variation on the technique just mentioned. The novel begins in the third person, but an anonymous and apparently heterodiegetic[15] first-person narrator soon enters: "Daban las once de la noche en el reloj de la plaza del General Orduña, ahora de Andalucía, cuando Lorenzo Quesada, corresponsal en *nuestra* ciudad... (7; emphasis added). Traces of this first-person narrator disappear almost entirely from the text, although there are subtle reminders of his presence: "[Quesada] colgó con disgusto el teléfono, aunque no con rabia, porque *es* un hombre de sentimientos extremadamente apacibles... (32; emphasis added). This use of the present tense suggests that the narrator knows Quesada personally: "Que no lo *dejen* comer a gusto o que le *priven* de nueve horas de sueño son las dos únicas razones que *pueden* alterar el carácter sosegado de Lorencito Quesada" (36; emphases added).

Due to the almost complete absence of personal pronouns referring to the narrator, the text of *Los misterios de Madrid* gives the overall impression of third-person narration until the final chapter, when the narrator suprises readers by entering the story as a character:

> Empujó [Quesada] la puerta de cristales, que hizo sonar una campanilla.
> Y es en ese momento cuando tiene entrada en esta historia mi humilde persona. Trabajo de mancebo en la farmacia Mataró... (186)

The story ends as Quesada begins telling the narrator his adventures with the opening words of the novel: "Daban las once en el reloj de la plaza del General Orduña..." (188). As in *El invierno de Lisboa*, the story is seen to be the work of not one but two narrators, with Quesada's pompous and hackneyed prose style—which his narratee so admires—parodying the language of a nineteenth-century *folletín*.

Muñoz Molina's consistent use of a homodiegetic narrator in his novels serves to foreground both the difficulty of so-called "objective" narration and the role of the subject as a constant mediator in the representation of events. In *Beatus ille*, Solana may conceal himself behind a third-person voice, but he is eventually exposed as a narrator who relies not only on what Inés has told him, but also on his own imagination. In *El invierno en Lisboa*, the events are narrated through a doubly-subjective filter, for Biralbo tells his story to a clearly sympathetic narrator who then imaginatively reconstructs it. *Beltenebros* and *El dueño del secreto* are recounted directly by a participant, but both foreground the subjective mediation of the narrator's imagination and memory, while in *El jinete polaco* the third-person narration of the story of Don Mercurio has been pieced together by the oral accounts of a number of different narrators, each of whose versions has experienced the inevitable modifications of memory and imagination: Don Mercurio tells his story to Ramiro, who in turn tells it to Comandante Galaz, who in turn tells it to Nadia. In *Los misterios de Madrid*, memory plays only a minor role in mediating Lorencito Quesada's eye-witness account of events, but his pretentious elocution continually reminds the reader that the style of the nineteenth-century *folletín* has informed his literary imagination throughout the text.

On one occasion in *El invierno en Lisboa*, the narrator's conversation with Biralbo—presented in the past tense—is unexpectedly interrupted by a reflection in the present:

> Sigo escuchando la canción: como una historia que me han contado muchas veces agradezco cada pormenor, cada desgarradura y cada trampa que me tiende la música, distingo las voces simultáneas de la trompeta y del piano, casi las guío, porque a cada instante sé lo que en seguida va a sonar, *como si yo mismo fuera inventando la canción y la historia* a medida que la escucho… (83; emphasis added)

"Inventing…the story" is a precise description of the narrator's role, for although he is a character in the story and in theory limited to what he personally can observe or hear, he takes on omniscient privileges as he imagines Biralbo's story, and by doing so assumes the function of an extra-textual author. As Muñoz Molina has said, "construimos para los demás una vida como el novelista construye un personaje" (*La realidad de la ficción*

31). This identification of the narrator as an author-figure is a self-reflexive commentary on the imagination as a literary act, making *El invierno en Lisboa* a metafictional text in which both the narrator and characters use parodic references to film, most notably the movie *Casablanca*. Alone together in the Lady Bird, Lucrecia talks with Santiago:

>—Tócala otra vez. Tócala otra vez para mí.
>—Sam, dijo él, calculando la risa y la complicidad—. Samtiago Biralbo. (80)

In the following chapter I will discuss Muñoz Molina's use of metafictional strategies, not only to foreground the role of the visibly inventing author but to question traditional distinctions between reality and fiction.

Notes

1 From our twentieth-century perspective, the dichotomy between perception and imagination has tended to break down, prompting heated debates such as the one in the pages of *Critical Inquiry* between Murray Krieger and E. H. Gombrich. The former defends the view that the representation of reality is purely conventional, while Gombrich insists that there are objective standards by which reality can be visually represented.

2 The short stories "La poseída" and "La colina de los sacrificios" first appeared in *El País* on Dec. 31, 1987 and Oct. 30, 1988 respectively. They were later included in the anthology of short stories *Nada del otro mundo*.

3 See his newspaper articles "Cuando Onetti" and "La vida breve."

4 The name of Onetti's character Brausen, from the novel *La vida breve*, appears three times in *El jinete polaco* (15; 513; 576).

5 This phrase is taken from García Lorca's poem "Romance somnámbulo" ("La noche se puso ínitima/como una pequeña plaza").

6 "[N]acimos en una sociedad rural, de cultura oral" (Gómez 122).

7 For Gérard Genette, a homodiegetic narrator is one present as a character in the story s/he tells (*Narrative Discourse. An Essay in Method* 244–5).

8 "Circumstantiality, verisimilitude, and many more of the qualities which we recognize as identifying characteristics of realism in narrative are all natural functions of the eye-witness point of view" (Scholes and Kellogg 250).

9 "First-person narration is, then, always at least potentially unreliable, in that the narrator, with these human limitations of perception and memory and assessment, may easily have missed, forgotten or misconstrued certain incidents, words, or motives" (Riggan 19–20). Susan Lanser, in chapter 4 of *The Narrative Act*, makes necessary and useful distinctions between the axes of privilege (omniscience), referential status (verisimilitude) and mimetic authority (reliability). Wayne Booth distinguishes between deceptive and unreliable narration in *The Rhetoric of Fiction* (158–59). I am not suggesting that the use of an unreliable narrator—or any other type of narrator for that matter—is limited to a particular era. In fact, the unreliable narrator is also a

defining feature of the Spanish picaresque novel of the sixteenth and seventeenth centuries, reflecting the epistemological and ethical crises characteristic of the Baroque era (see Chapter 2 of Riggan).

[10] The narrator of *Fortunata y Jacinta* refers to himself as an "historiador" who must deliver "una relación verídica y grave" (I, 636).

[11] The case of a homodiegetic narrator who by suddenly becoming omniscient is able to focalize through another character is not exceptional, and is called "polymodality" by Genette (*Narrative Discourse. An Essay in Method* 198–211). Susan Lanser also refers to this curious but not uncommon strategy: "The conventions regulating the relationship between a narrator's privilege and the mode of representation are violated more frequently than one might expect.... [O]ne kind of deviation from the norm occurs when a homodiegetic narrator takes the omniscient privilege of the heterodiegetic voice" (162).

[12] Genette uses the term "focalization" "[t]o avoid the too specifically visual connotations of the terms *vision, field,* and *point of view*" (*Narrative Discourse. An Essay in Method* 189; author's emphases). Rimmon-Kenan insists that the term "is not free of optical-photographic connotations" and proposes that "its purely visual sense has to be broadened to include cognitive, emotive and ideological orientation" (71). I have used the term in this broader sense.

[13] It is significant that while contrasting first-person to third-person narration—purely grammatical categories—Muñoz Molina also addresses the presence or absence of the narrator in the story, a question of narrative levels. Genette states that "[t]he novelist's choice, unlike the narrator's, is not between two grammatical forms, but between two narrative postures (whose grammatical forms are simply an automatic consequence): to have the story told by one of its 'characters,' or to have it told by a narrator outside of the story" (*Narrative Discourse. An Essay in Method* 244). When Muñoz Molina refers to "el ángulo donde ha de situarse la mirada" (*La realidad de la ficción* 63), he alludes to yet another aspect of discourse—what narratologists like Genette and others refer to as "focalization." Although Muñoz Molina may not always distinguish theoretically between grammatical voice, narrative level and focalization, as a practicing writer of fiction he appears to be intuitively well aware of these differences.

[14] See Muñoz Molina's article "Un santuario para Bill Faulkner." When asked about his literary preferences, he mentioned *Absalom,*

Absalom! as one of his favorite novels: "Para mí…son insustituibles: *El Quijote, Absalón, Absalón,* de Faulkner, *Una educación sentimental,* de Flaubert, *Si te dicen que caí,* de Juan Marsé" (*El Independiente* 19 Aug. 1990: 54).

15 For Gérard Genette, a heterodiegetic narrator is one absent from the story s/he tells (*Narrative Discourse. An Essay in Method* 244–5).

Chapter Two

History and Metafiction

> yo era un lento fantasma que fingía que iba a matar a un hombre y se internaba en la mentira como en una selva de espejismos. (*Beltenebros*)

For centuries, Western thought has conceived of history and fiction as two distinct and separate categories. According to Hayden White, traditional criticism has used history "as a kind of archetype of the 'realistic' pole of representation" ("Historical" 288), and has refused to recognize that

> the distinction, as old as Aristotle, between history and poetry obscures as much as it illuminates about both. If there is an element of the historical in all poetry, there is an element of poetry in every historical account of the world. (300)

White points out that historical narratives are "verbal fictions…the forms of which have more in common with their counterparts in literature than they have with those in the sciences" (278). Because "real events do not offer themselves as stories" ("The Value" 4), historical writing is similar to fictional writing in that it attempts to endow events with meaning through narrativization. However, narrativization implies the use of figurative language ("Historical" 295), and White proposes that

> [t]he older distinction between fiction and history, in which fiction is conceived as the representation of the imaginable and history as the representation of the actual, must give place to the recognition that we can only know the *actual* by contrasting it with or likening it to the *imaginable*. (300; author's emphases)

A genre that clearly demonstrates a synthesis of history and the literary imagination is epic poetry, for a text like the *Poema de Mío Cid* can be read not only as fiction but also as an invaluable record of the past. Consequently, scholars like Menéndez Pidal have treated it as a historical document which details the exploits of a real figure, Don Rodrigo de Vivar. However, in order to glorify Rodrigo as a national hero of the Reconquest, his portrayal both in the *Poema de Mío Cid* and in Alfonso X's *Estoria de España* and other chronicles takes on mythical and fantastic dimensions. This tendency to mythicize a historical figure is a common phenomenon and a subject which Muñoz Molina treats in both *Beatus ille* and *Beltenebros*.

In *Myth and History in the Contemporary Spanish Novel*, Jo Labanyi describes how Spanish fascism propagated a mythical view of Spain based on the desire for a return to authentic origins and eternal values.[1] Rejecting what was perceived as the decadence of progressive social change, Nationalist ideology embraced the myth of an eternal and unchanging Spain, a concept acquired in part from '98 writers like Ganivet and Unamuno. However, Labanyi also notes that writers opposed to the Franco regime unwittingly fell into adopting a similar mythical perspective:

> the new generation of opposition novelists that emerged in the 1950s would preach the need for social realism...but in practice produced works with strong mythical undertones.... [W]hat is surprising is that Delibes' evocation of a Paradise Lost and Cela's cyclical vision recur in the work of younger writers such as Jesús Fernández Santos, Rafael Sánchez Ferlosio, and the brothers Juan and Luis Goytisolo.... The difference is, of course, that the Falange identified the Fall with progress and looked back to the Paradise Lost of traditional values, whereas the novels of the 1950s identify the Fall with Nationalist victory and look back to the Paradise Lost of the Republic. (41–42; 44)

Labanyi's view of myth as a common denominator in postwar fiction is echoed by David Herzberger, who writes that Francoist historians and social realists used essentially the same mythical mode of discourse: "the mythic foundations of both discourses are bound up by the same narrative assumptions" ("Narrating the Past" 37). Herzberger proposes that the "novel of memory" characteristic of a new generation of writers—including the later Juan Goytisolo—offers a new vision of history, for it "differs from social realistic fiction in stripping history of its structured oneness, of its mythical enactment of progression..." (37)[2]. Although Herzberger does not mention Muñoz Molina's work in his discussion of the novel of memory, he might well have included *Beatus ille* and *Beltenebros*, for in both novels the mythical foundations of Francoist historiography and social realist narrative are challenged. I will first address the way in which *Beatus ille* aims to dispel one prevalent postwar myth: that of the heroic poet militantly dedicated to the Republican cause.

For anti-Francoists, poets like Rafael Alberti and Miguel Hernández were—and for many Spaniards still are—revered symbols of the opposition to fascism, historical figures who attained an almost mythical stature. This phenomenon was unwittingly abetted by Francoist censorship, for the very fact that a book or magazine had been banned for political reasons gave it the aura of a sacred text. When Luque approaches Minaya in the university cafeteria, he is carrying photocopies of *Hora de España* and *El Mono Azul*, two Republican magazines published between 1936 and 1938, the first of which has been called "un tramo importante de la mitología de la guerra civil" (Mainer, *La edad* 338). The pages are described as "frágiles, sagradas como reliquias, como los manuscritos de una fe perseguida y oculta, grávidas de *memoria heroica* y de conspiración" (*Beatus ille* 19; emphasis added). Luque is an unequivocal believer in Solana's mythical stature, viewing him as both "prestigioso" and "heroico" (18).

Of the poems that Luque has with him, Minaya first reads one by Solana entitled "Invitación," which is not a politically-inspired *romance* but "una tranquila invitación al suicidio" composed of "quince versos sin rima, sin ningún ritmo evidente" (18). He then reads Solana's *romances* and notes that the poet's voice "ya no era la misma que había escuchado...cuando leyó el primer poema," as if "el hombre que había escrito los romances no fuera el mismo..." (19). Minaya's reading of the first poem suggests that Solana is perhaps not the heroic Republican rebel whom Luque has envisioned. Indeed, another view of Solana begins to emerge in Part II, as Manuel recalls Solana telling Utrera:

> Recordé con vergüenza todas las cosas que yo había escrito, los artículos en *El Sol* y en *Octubre*, los romances en el *Mono Azul* y en los murales de guerra, y me di cuenta de que necesitaba romperlo y olvidarlo todo para escribir algo que se pareciera a las acuarelas de Orlando. (127)

When Minaya finally meets Solana, the latter tells him that he had begun writing for surrealist and "vanguardista" periodicals, but

> de pronto estábamos en la guerra y ya no quedaba tiempo ni justificación moral para otra cosa que no fuera la fabricación metódica de romances contra el fascismo y de piezas de teatro que algunas veces vi representar por los frentes con una sensación de vergüenza y de fraude tan intensa y tan inconfesable como la que me producía verme vestido con un mono azul entre los milicianos.... Beatriz me dijo que yo no había creído nunca

> ni en la República ni el comunismo…que si en el verano del 37 me alisté de soldado…no fue para combatir con las armas a los fascistas, sino para buscar la muerte que no me atrevía a darme a mí mismo. (271)

Solana then informs Minaya that he is not such a noble figure as the latter imagined him to be, saying "usted…vino aquí para buscar un libro y un misterio y la biografía de un héroe" (276), but "ha sido en su imaginación donde hemos vuelto a nacer, mucho mejores que lo que fuimos, más leales y más hermosos, limpios de la cobardía y de la verdad" (278). *Beatus ille* dispels the myth of the *engagé* poet by having Solana himself reveal his human frailties, his artistic reservations, and his ambivalent attitude towards the Republican cause.

Despite the qualification of Solana's heroism in *Beatus ille*, the ideology of the implied author is clearly one of sympathy for the Republicans.[3] This is evident in the negative portrayal of Franco's regime—which imprisoned Solana for eight years—and of the two Nationalist sympathizers Doña Elvira and Utrera, Mariana's murderer. However, the novel avoids a Manichean view of the Civil War, for it also implicitly condemns the lynching of a Nationalist, which Solana witnesses in the Plaza del General Orduña. Most importantly, however, it challenges the myth of Solana as a one-dimensional hero.

Like *Beatus ille*, *Beltenebros* is a novel in which the implied author is clearly identified with the Republican cause. The police commissioner, Beltenebros, is depicted as an incarnation of evil, and one of his pseudonyms, Valdivia, refers to the Spanish *conquistador* Pedro de Valdivia whom Pablo de Neruda portrays as a ruthless executioner in his *Canto general*.[4] However, in *Beltenebros* Muñoz Molina also takes a critical look at certain myths of the anti-Franco resistance. One of these was the mistaken notion held by certain members of the Spanish Communist Party (PCE) that the people would soon rise up to overthrow the dictatorship, allowing political exiles to return to a democratic Spain. In Chapter 1, Darman reflects on the resistance members in exile:

> [E]ra así como actuaban siempre, fingiendo que gentes enemigas y espías los asediaban y que a pesar de la conspiración universal urdida contra ellos estaban culminando los episodios de una sublevación definitiva. (12)

> No les debía nada ni me apetecía reclamarles nada, ni siquiera el tiempo que había gastado secundando sus fantasmagorías de conspiración y vengativo regreso. (19)

When Darman tells Walter that the Allies will aid the Spanish resistance—"Todo va a cambiar ahora que ha terminado la guerra en Europa.... Los aliados nos ayudarán" (116)—he is aware that he is simply mouthing the belief of his superiors, and interjects: "oí mi voz como si fuera la de uno de esos locutores de la radio."[5] Walter predicts what actually would occur, saying that the Allies will do nothing to ameliorate the plight of the Spanish people: "Les importamos menos que una tribu de Africa" (117).

Luque—who in *Beatus ille* envisions Solana as "heroico"—reappears in *Beltenebros*, where he is depicted as religiously idealizing the members of the anti-Franco resistance, including Darman: "había conocido a los héroes y era su discípulo..." (31). Luque reads Russian revolutionary manuals "no para aprender nada...sino para ingresar imaginariamente en la comunión de los héroes" (38). After executing Andrade, Darman remarks that Luque "ya se contaba a sí mismo en el número de los héroes" (182–3), unaware that he has murdered a man who was simply a pawn of the real traitor, Beltenebros. Likewise, Darman is not the hero whom Luque believes him to be, for Darman has also executed an innocent man, Walter. Andrade's death is thus a reminder that in the struggle between the Left and the Right no one has survived morally untainted, and his blood symbolically stains both Luque and Darman (183). Parallel to the way in which *Beatus ille* demythicizes Solana, *Beltenebros* also challenges the myth of the heroic and virtuous resistance leader.[6]

In both *Beatus ille* and *Beltenebros*, Muñoz Molina questions what is generally accepted as historical "fact" by foregrounding the very process of history-making as his characters attempt to recover the past. If one conceives of history as a record of past events, it is a *sine qua non* that to be recounted or recorded these events must first be witnessed. *Beatus ille* underscores this by depicting situations in which an eye-witness is lacking. Because shots were heard the night that Mariana was killed, it is assumed that she was killed in the cross-fire between the Republican militia and a Nationalist *faccioso* who was attempting to escape, although no one actually witnessed her death. Similarly, Solana is presumed to have been killed by the Guardia Civil, but again, not one character has witnessed his death. The housekeeper of Manuel's country estate, Frasco, is described as *"testigo* de los últimos días y de la muerte de Solana" (99; emphasis added), but when Minaya interviews him, Frasco admits that "Yo no lo vi. Sólo lo vieron ellos, los que lo mataron" (101). And ironically, when Manuel is summoned to identify Solana's corpse, he is convinced that it is Solana because he recognizes the latter's eyeglasses and clothes. However, Manuel does not bother to look at the body's face—"Retrocedió...sin mirar el rostro deshecho..." (184)—and fails to see that it is not in fact the poet's body. As Muñoz Molina writes, "la mirada miente y las apariencias engañan" ("La manera de vivir").

When characters have not witnessed an event, they will often resort to their imagination to reconstruct it. *Beatus ille* is replete with situations in which an event has never been witnessed, prompting characters to imagine or invent what they presume has occurred. When Solana decides to tell his fiancée, María Teresa, that he wishes to break off their engagement, no one is present:

> Manuel se presentó en casa de la señorita López Cabaña...y, luego de pedir a la madre y a las hermanas *que lo dejaran solo con su prometida*... (140; emphasis added)

As I have proposed in the previous chapter, the imagination is an intertextual faculty often informed by fiction. Consequently, the fact that no one witnesses the meeting between Solana and María Teresa does not prevent the townspeople of Mágina from creating a dramatic but purely imaginary scene based on their knowledge of *folletines*. In this scene, both the narrator's commentary and the word "acaso" underscore the story's conditional status as an imaginary narrative:

> este añadido escena era, por supuesto, falso...se sentó junto a ella, le ofreció las violetas con la impecable sonrisa de un impostor...mirando acaso sus propias manos... (140)

A character need not invent a scene s/he has not witnessed to arrive at a false or distorted version of events. Repeatedly, characters are depicted as relying on information that has been given to them by others. When Solana's wife meets him after his release from prison, she says:

> Una mujer *me dijo* que *le habían dicho* que *te vieron* enfermo o herido en el campo de Argelés, pero también *decían* que habías huido hacia el mar y que te hicieron preso en el puerto de Alicante. (119; emphases added)

This muddled version of Solana's capture exemplifies the etymology of the word "hearsay," and when Manuel says "Sé, me han dicho, que el segundo o el tercer día de abril de 1939 lo vieron llegar" (144), the danger of accepting others' versions of events is likewise emphasized. These and similar situations recall the children's game in which a sentence is whispered successively from one person to another, and which always results in a final version that is significantly different from the original.

Like *Beatus ille*, *Beltenebros* also underscores the role of the imagination in supplanting direct observation: "Vine a Madrid para matar a un hombre *a quien no había visto nunca*" (7; emphasis added). Darman must imagine Andrade waiting in the abandoned warehouse at Atocha: "me esperó disciplinadamente, muerto de frío, supongo, y de aburrimiento y tal vez de terror…" (7). When the commissar Beltenebros arrives at the warehouse, Darman hides behind a curtain, where he can only imagine the scene between Beltenebros and Rebeca Osorio:

> Yo no veía nada y lo escuchaba todo…y cuanto más hondo averiguaba que él estaba rozando con sus blandas manos de fiebre más convulsa y más aguda se volvía su respiración, y más ahogadas sus palabras, que tal vez ni él mismo oía, rígido, imaginé… (77–8)

The dramatic conclusion of *Beatus ille* achieves its effect because both the characters and the reader are led to believe that Solana is dead, although nobody in fact witnessed his execution. This same strategy is employed in *Beltenebros*, for Darman believes that Valdivia was executed when in fact he is alive in the person of Beltenebros. Darman belives that "Valdivia fue detenido y atormentado y murió sin denunciar a nadie. Lo fusilaron maniatado a una silla…" (130–1), but only because he has been told so by others. However, his superiors are mistaken not only about Valdivia's death but also about Andrade's guilt. Bernal tells Darman "tenemos pruebas. Pruebas indudables" (29), but the evidence incriminating Andrade proves to have been wrongly interpreted. Darman's primary error is relying on what can only be called hearsay, and he is ultimately powerless to save Andrade's life, discovering too late that he is not the real traitor whom Bernal has been pursuing.

A fundamental aspect of defining history as a record of the past is the question of time. Not only is there a temporal gap between the recording of events and their reception—we read histories after they are written—but events are also generally recounted *a posteriori* by a subject who must retain what s/he has witnessed until recording it. The accuracy of an historical account depends in part on the memory of witnesses, and the characters in both *Beatus ille* and *Beltenebros* are not only unable to recall key events but also confuse what they imagine with what they remember. As I have already noted, Muñoz Molina often equates the mental faculties of memory and imagination—logically so, for if to recall events from the past is to create a mental image of them, to recall *is* in one sense to imag(in)e. The characters in *Beatus ille* repeatedly use the terms memory and imagination interchangeably. When Solana returns to Mágina, he tells Manuel that during his years in prison he did not let himself forget the interior of Manuel's house, saying "Me gustaba imaginarlo todo. Me imponía la disciplina de recordar todas las cosas con absoluta exactitud" (124–5). Similarly, Utrera is described as "recordando o inventando..." (39).

The conflation of memory and imagination serves in *Beatus ille* to call into question the foundations of historical knowledge. If history is a record *a posteriori* of remembered events, it is ultimately dependent on memory's subjectivity, and this is continually underscored in *Beatus ille*. When Minaya meets his uncle Manuel, "recordaba una alta figura de pelo gris...pero el rostro...se había borrado siempre en su memoria" and he discovers that Manuel "[e]ra mucho menos alto que en los recuerdos..." (23). Similarily, when Solana meets his wife Beatriz after eight years in prison, he describes her as "más alta de lo que yo recordaba..." (118). Manuel thinks so much about his dead bride that "de tanto pensar en Mariana...se le gastaron los recuerdos" (25), and Minaya reflects: "[n]o dura la memoria..." (103).

Memory in *Beltenebros* signifies for Darman a means of either reconstructing or rejecting history. The protagonist has spent so long as an exile that his past in Spain has become unreal to him: "Uno cree que los lugares y los rostros dejan de existir cuando no los recuerda" (190). It is not that Darman *cannot* remember his execution of Walter—"el oprobio de una cruda desgracia interminablemente recordada" (13)—but that he does not *want* to, and he underscores this by telling Luque "Yo todavía no me acordaba de su nombre, o no quería" (44).[7] Darman attempts to feign his emotional distance from the past by saying of Walter "Nunca me arrepentí de matarlo. Olvidé su cara y su nombre..." (140), although he confesses that "Cada vez que volvía a Madrid era como si perdiese la piel de la indiferencia y olvido que el tiempo había agregado a la memoria..." (60). By returning to Spain, Darman is forced to relivir through memory his years as a member of the anti-Franco resistance.

In *Beltenebros*, the characters' inability to remember is also instrumental in furthering the plot. Darman's forgetfulness puts him into several dramatic situations, as when he barely escapes death by failing to recognize the doorman of the *Boite Tabú* as the hunchback who had worked at the

Universal Cinema. Even Darman's short-term memory is faulty, for after only a few hours in his hotel room he goes down to the reception desk to find that "[v]isto desde otro ángulo, el vestíbulo del hotel no era exactamente como yo lo recordaba…" (37). Rebeca Osorio is unable to remember her father—"Nunca me acuerdo de su cara, ni de su voz" (166)—and consequently is unaware that he is the police commissioner, Beltenebros.

In *Beatus ille* and *Beltenebros*, the characters' attempts to recover the past are constantly hindered by situations in which the three faculties of observation, imagination, and memory fail to aid the characters in their search for historical truth. Witnesses are often absent or unreliable, characters misinterpret or imagine what they have or have not seen, and memory falters or deceives. This emphasis on epistemological uncertainty is characteristic of Muñoz Molina's fiction, and is used self-consciously in his novels to emphasize that what we think of as history is often a mere fiction.

Metafiction

In the late 1960s, literary critics began to take note of an increasing self-consciousness manifested in works by contemporary novelists. Although both John Barth and Robert Scholes discussed this trend in two seminal articles published in 1967 and 1970 respectively,[8] Robert Alter's *Partial Magic* (1975) was the first important full-length study of what he called in the book's subtitle "the novel as a self-conscious genre." For Alter, a self-conscious novel is

> a novel that systematically flaunts its own condition of artifice and that by so doing probes into the problematic relationship between real-seeming artifice and reality. (x)

Although history has been traditionally conceived of as a "discourse of the real" in contrast to the imaginative discourses of fiction, writers from Cervantes on have attempted to subvert this dichotomy by using historical themes as the basis for self-conscious texts, also called "metafictions."[9] This is the case in *Beatus ille* and *Beltenebros*, for they not only question the distinction between history and fiction from within their diegetic worlds by demythicizing the figure of the heroic anti-Francoist, but also point to their own status as fictions by problematizing the role of the narrator.

There are many different ways in which a text may "flaunt" (Alter) or "draw attention to" (Waugh) its status as fiction. Following Linda Hutcheon's typology, *Beatus ille* is "diegetically self-conscious" in that it draws attention to the act of narration itself.[10] Although the novel's narrative technique is highly complex, complete with temporal analepses and swiftly changing focalization, the story content is essentially realistic, for in addition to historically-based temporal and spatial references, the characters (though perhaps somewhat lacking in psychological profundity) are verisimilar[11] and correspond to a number of immediately recognizable types: hundreds of students like Minaya were incarcerated by Franco's secret police after university demonstrations, aging aristocrats like Manuel were not uncommon in Spain's provincial towns and cities in the 1960s and '70s, and the fictional figure of Solana is modelled on real civil war poets like Miguel Hernández to whom Solana compares himself.[12] Muñoz Molina himself admitted in an interview that *Beatus ille* "tenía mucho de realismo" (Rich 1992). However, *Beatus ille* is also a self-conscious text that utilizes a problematic narrator, for rather than guaranteeing the reader's unconditional acceptance of a fictional world, the mysterious narrator—who is later revealed to be Solana—serves to highlight the fact that "historical" or "impersonal" narration is an illusion. *Beatus ille* is thus both realistic and metafictional in that it carries an explicit commentary on its own narrative process by foregrounding the role of a subjective narrator. As critics have stressed, realism and metafiction are not necessarily incompatible—David Lodge notes that "it would be false to oppose metafiction to realism; rather, metafiction makes explicit the implicit problematic of realism" (19), and Patricia Waugh agrees: "Metafiction explicitly lays bare the conventions of realism; it does not ignore or abandon them" (18).

The opening scene of *Beatus ille* is a room in Mágina from which an unidentified voice begins narrating, describing both the room and the night outside:

> la habitación ha quedado en sombras, y ahora sólo me alumbra el hilo de luz que viene del corredor...pero en la ventana hay una noche azul oscura y por sus postigos abiertos viene un aire de noche próxima al verano y cruzada desde muy lejos por las sirenas de los expresos... (7)

The voice that refers to itself as an "I" immediately oversteps the traditional physical limitations of a homodiegetic narrator and informs the reader that Minaya is waiting for Inés at the train station. Since the narrator cannot see Minaya, he imagines the scene and uses the conditional expression "tal vez" to describe it: "él, Minaya, la está esperando ahora mismo.... Está solo, sentado en un banco, fumando tal vez mientras mira las luces rojas..." (7).

The narrator's transgression of eye-witness limitations is then self-consciously flaunted as he says "puedo, si quiero, imaginarlo todo...puedo imaginar o contar lo que ha sucedido...como si en este instante los inventara y dibujara su presencia, su deseo y su culpa" (7–8). He deliberately portrays himself as an omniscient creator of fictions, one who can direct the characters' actions as if they were mere puppets. As he says of Inés:

> Basta mi conciencia y la soledad y las palabras que pronuncio en voz baja *para guiarla* camino de la calle y de la estación donde él no sabe no seguir esperándola. Ya no es preciso escribir para adivinar o *inventar las cosas*. (8; emphases added)

With its use of the terms "guide" and "invent," this passage offers a parallel to the one previously cited from *El invierno en Lisboa*:

> distingo las voces simultáneas de la trompeta y del piano, casi las guío, porque a cada instante sé lo que en seguida va a sonar, como si yo mismo fuera inventando la canción y la historia a medida que la escucho... (83)

The first-person narrator of *Beatus ille*—initially presented as homodiegetic—then begins to alternate with an omniscient third-person voice, which as I noted previously is a technique used by nineteenth-century realist authors. The third-person narrator focalizes through the other characters, beginning with Minaya:

> Desde la plaza, tras los árboles, como un viajero casual, *Minaya mira* la arquitectura de la casa, *dudando* todavía ante los llamadores de bronce.... Losas de mármol, *recuerda*.... En aquel tiempo *Minaya percibía* las cosas con una claridad muy parecida al asombro.... Porque *advertía* la hostilidad de su madre hacia aquella casa... (9–10; emphases added)

The narrator's "I" returns only once at the end of chapter 1 and disappears completely in chapter 2, which is focalized entirely through Minaya as we are informed of the events leading up to his decision to return to Mágina. This strategy gives the impression of "personal" narration:

> Minaya [yo] estaba solo...y aún no se [me] había acordado de Jacinto Solana...[yo] sólo pensaba...en interrogatorios y sirenas de furgonetas.... [Yo] Veía en torno suyo [mío] rostros desconocidos... (16)

However, focalization in *Beatus ille* is not confined to Minaya, and throughout the text extensive passages narrated in the third person also allow access to the thoughts and sensations of Manuel.

In *Beatus ille*, the first-person narrator who seldom refers to himself produces an effect of almost phantasmic absence, a condition of disembodied voice to which he clearly aspires: "puedo, si quiero, imaginarlo todo para mí solo, es decir, para *nadie*..." (7; emphasis added). Solana later tells Minaya that he has chosen "el privilegio de ser otro hombre o de ser nadie" (275), echoing a similar statement by the author's Urban Robinson who longs for "el privilegio de la inexistencia, el no ser nadie" (*El Robinson urbano* 136). Being "nobody" not only refers to Solana's physical seclusion in Mágina, but is also a self-conscious flaunting of his ability to conceal himself as a narrator behind a third-person voice. This implicit commentary on the nineteenth-century convention of the alternating first- and third-person narrator is made explicit in Solana's diary:

> A veces Solana escribía en primera persona, y otras veces usaba la tercera como si quisiera ocultar la voz que lo contaba y lo adivinaba todo, para dar así a la narración el tono de una crónica impasible. (89)

Although Solana self-consciously adapts the nineteenth-century convention of an alternating first and third-person voice, there is a clear difference between him and his realist counterpart. The narrator of *Fortunata y Jacinta*—like his *costumbrista* predecessors—walks the streets of Madrid as an observer of events, and when he speaks in the first person, he relates only what he has been able to observe ("He visto" [238]) or what he has been told by people he knows personally ("cuenta Villalonga" [99]). As a character in the story, he confesses to his limitations in order to assure the reader of his reliability ("Esto sí que no lo sé" [110]), and his omniscient abilities are reserved exclusively for a third-person voice. However, Solana is an invalid confined to his room, which he leaves only once to attend Manuel's funeral. Since Solana's only source of information is Inés, apart from what she tells him ("Dijo Inés" [21, 33, 47, 86]) he must rely solely on his memory and imagination rather than on observation, emphasizing that what he is narrating is a fiction: "Debo imaginarlo" (32); "lo imagino" (77); "no sé si al escribir estoy contando lo que sucedió entonces o únicamente imagino" (176); "Puedo recordar...veo o muy probablemente imagino" (194).

Another fundamental difference between Solana and the Galdosian narrator is that the latter's use of a third-person voice aids the mimetic illusion of a text in which "the events seem to narrate themselves" (Benveniste 208), and as a first-person narrator he is never allowed to interfere with, or unduly influence, the events of the story. In contrast, although Solana is initially anonymous, the surprise ending exposes him as a character in the story, the events of which he himself has controlled by planting physical clues for Minaya. And given that he has narrated the story in which he himself is a character, a metafictional situation arises, one analogous to Escher's hand that draws itself. Solana's violation of the conventional boundary that exists between the level of discourse and the level of story is a technique described by Robert Spires in his definition of the metafictional mode:

> If we accept the fictional mode as a triad consisting of the world of the fictive author, the world of the story, and the world of the text-act reader...a metafictional mode results when the member of one world violates the world of another.... Such violations of the boundaries separating these three worlds, boundaries that have come to be accepted as sacred conventions of fiction, call attention to the arbitrariness of the conventions and thereby unmask any illusion that what is being narrated is real rather than mere fiction. (*Beyond the Metafictional Mode* 15–16)

As a diegetically self-conscious text, *Beatus ille* demonstrates that so-called "impersonal" or "historical" narration is an illusion, for third-person narration always implies the existence of an enunciating subject. By concealing himself behind a third-person voice, Solana maintains the illusion of historical narration until the surprise conclusion, when by erupting into the text he informs the reader that he has controlled events from the start, both as character and as narrator. As he tells Minaya, "concebí el juego, igual que si se me ocurriera de pronto el argumento de un libro" (276).[13]

Like *Beatus ille*, *Beltenebros* is a metafiction, although the two texts have little in common stylistically. *Beatus ille* employs both first- and third-person narration, whereas *Beltenebros* is recounted exclusively in the first person by Darman. In addition, *Beltenebros* avoids most of the nineteenth-century realist conventions used in *Beatus ille*, such as references to real figures (Alfonso XIII, Pedro Salinas, Miguel Hernández, Luis Buñuel), detailed accounts of a character's past (Manuel, Solana, Minaya, Utrera), and the frequent use of dates to situate events historically. In contrast, the characters of *Beltenebros* are portrayed without a personal past, and there are fewer dates mentioned. This approach to characterization and temporal vagueness has led one critic to comment disapprovingly:

> Los personajes no logran librarse de su apariencia de actores.... [L]a localización temporal de la novela no result[a] claro. Mientras que algunos datos hacen pensar en el final de los años sesenta, otros, tranvías, sombreros, nos remiten a la década de los cincuenta. (Bértolo 15)

By trying to make *Beltenebros* conform to the model of a realist text, Bértolo has in my opinion failed to understand that the novel consciously aims at temporal indeterminacy and allegorical abstraction. As the author said in an interview:

> Quería hacer una especie de fábula abstracta, que funcionara como fábula abstracta, ¿sabes? Y de hecho, de eso estoy contento, de esa parte, de ese tono estoy contento. No se dice nunca la palabra "partido" ni la palabra "comunismo." (Rich 1992)

In another interview, Muñoz Molina explained that he avoided explicit historical references "porque ese material había que convertirlo en épica, en literatura, en ficción" (Vidal-Folch). Nevertheless, the astute reader with some knowledge of Spanish history will be able to establish a rough temporal framework for the events in the novel.

Both the characters and the world of *Beltenebros* are deliberately represented as strange and unfamiliar by Darman, who constantly points out the unreality of the people and places he sees. Luque "pareció desvanecerse como una sombra sin cuerpo" (28), a cathedral seen from a hotel window is "tan irreal y cercana como un espejismo" (28), and the streets of Madrid are "las calles de un Madrid irreal" (156). Darman emphasizes the fictional content of memory—the events of his past "tenían una irrealidad de pasado lejano" (143)—and he refers to his own existence as illusory and unreal by saying "sentí que estaba transitando de una vida hacia otra, y que ninguna de las dos era verdad" (152–3). The text is saturated with references to the narrator's sense of his inhabiting a world of fiction:

> la ficción...me guiaba como un impulso que suspende las leyes de la gravedad y de la verosimilitud, pues desde que acepté viajar a Madrid yo era un lento fantasma que fingía que iba a matar a un hombre y se internaba en la mentira como en una selva de espejismos. (56–7)

These commentaries on the fictive nature of people and events include explicit references to pulp fiction and the equally fictional world of film:

> En las novelas que [Rebeca Osorio] escribió durante algunos años, como en el nombre que usaba para firmarlas, había un ensañamiento en la

inverosimilitud y la parodia que yo creía copiado de los melodramas del cine y que ella atribuía al azar diario de la vida. (85)

Beltenebros is a self-conscious novel which uses Rebeca Osorio's novels as a *mise en abîme* of the text itself, for the characters are portrayed to be as fictional as those whom Rebeca invents. On seeing Rebeca, Darman notes that she dresses like her characters—"Así se vestían y miraban las heroínas de las novelas de Rebeca Osorio" (160)—and her face "tenía la misma palidez que las imágenes del cine..." (87). The cinematic quality of both people and places is often emphasized—Darman's hotel room is "una habitacíon tan alta y tan estrecha que parecía tener sólo dos dimensiones" (23) and Rebeca is "como una figura sin volumen" (160). Darman feels "como si nada tuviera un volumen firme de verdad, ni yo mismo" (213), and he speaks of "el Madrid en blanco y negro del pasado" (219). As a self-conscious parody of *film noir*, *Beltenebros* accentuates the "flatness" of its characters as if they were actors on a screen.

Bértolo's negative appraisal of *Beltenebros* cited above and Leopoldo Azancot's statement that the characters of *El invierno en Lisboa* "son de cartón piedra" reflect a persistent attempt by some critics to apply nineteenth-century realist standards to what are evidently metafictional texts.[14] However, although *Beltenebros* is given a historical setting, it should be read as a metafiction which deliberately flaunts the fictive nature of its scenes and characters: "What is immediately postulated as axiomatic in such fiction is the fictiveness of the referents of the text's language" (Hutcheon, "Metafictional" 2).

In *The Poetics of Postmodernism*, Linda Hutcheon defines "historiographic metafiction" as fiction that

> problematize[s] both the nature of the referent and its relation to the real, historical world by its paradoxical combination of metafictional self-reflexivity with historical subject matter. (19)

She stresses that historiographic metafiction "does not deny the *existence* of the past; it does question whether we can ever *know* that past other than through its textualized remains" (20; author's emphases). In accord with Hutcheon's model, *Beatus ille* and *Beltenebros* are historiographic metafictions that do not deny the reality of the Spanish Civil War and its aftermath of political repression, but *do* attempt to question how that past has been interpreted. In doing so, both novels challenge the myth of the heroic and militant anti-Francoist, in marked contrast to the one-sided view of history offered by the literature of social realism.

According to Hutcheon, historiographic metafictions privilege two modes of narration: multiple points of view or an overtly controlling narrator (*Poetics* 117). She notes that "[i]n neither, however, do we find a subject confident of his/her ability to know the past with any certainty" (117) for "we are epistemologically limited in our ability to know that past, since we are both spectators of and actors in the historical process" (122). By choosing Solana and Darman as narrators, Muñoz Molina underscores the impossibility of what Solana calls "una crónica impasible," for both are actors and spectators of their own (hi)story and demonstrate the inevitably contingent and subjective status of historical narration.

Hutcheon also notes that in re-presenting the past, historical metafictions "open it up to the present, to prevent it from being conclusive and teleological" (110). At the end of *Beatus ille*, Solana says to Minaya:

> acaso la historia que usted ha encontrado sólo es una entre varias posibles. Tal vez había otros manuscritos en la casa o en "La Isla de Cuba", y el azar ha hecho que usted no diera con ellos. (277)

The past is not denied—Solana says "no inventé la muerte de Mariana ni la culpa de Utrera" (276)—but no final and definitive version is offered. Throughout *Beltenebros*, Darman is characterized by his inability to discover the truth, and the title *(Bel)tenebro(u)s* alludes to his condition of being—in the words of a popular expression—constantly "in the dark" about matters. Even the apparent closure that *Beltenebros* effects with the discovery and death of the police commissioner leaves a certain ambiguity around the facts surrounding Andrade's and Walter's supposed betrayal of the organization headed by Bernal.[15] Thus, although *Beatus ille* and *Beltenebros* both challenge historical myths, they do not pretend to erect a counter-myth or offer a "true" version of Spanish history. As Solana tells Minaya, "No importa que una historia sea verdad o mentira, sino que uno sepa contarla" (277).

Muñoz Molina has not confined his use of metafictional strategies to texts based on historical themes. One example is "Borrador de una historia," a short story about an author of pulp fiction, Frank Blatsky. It is written entirely in the third person, and is initially focalized through the protagonist with frequent use of indirect free style. Blatsky has lost his job at a newspaper and spends his time in a rented office writing pulp fiction of all types, although his preference is for detective novels. He draws on everything from pornographic magazines to personal advice columns for inspiration, and like many of Muñoz Molina's characters spends his time fantasizing: "Llega cada mañana a las nueve y se queda mirando la calle, las mujeres, los autobuses, imaginando historias... (*Nada del otro mundo* 194).

One day Blatsky begines to imagine a detective whose name, Blázquez, he has seen on a plaque in the entrance hall of an old building. He pictures what the detective might be doing at that moment: "Acaso ese mismo detective, Blázquez, que ahora, a las nueve de la mañana, se estará aburriendo en la penumbra de su oficina..." (195). As Blatsky imagines the detective buying his novels, the focalization shifts to Blázquez:

> Anda [Blázquez] despacio por la calle, con las manos en los bolsillos, mirando a las mujeres, mirando en los quioscos las revistas obscenas y los semanarios de crímenes, comprando alguna vez.... Ultimamente prefiere las de un tipo llamado F. Blatsky: seguro que es un pseudónimo, nadie que escriba novelas puede llamarse así. A lo mejor se lo puso porque le da vergüenza escribir tanta basura... (196)

After Blázquez imagines Blatsky's life, Blatsky imagines Blázquez's—indicated by the demonstrative "este" instead of "ese" and confirmed by the phrase "piensa sentado:"

> Qué ignominia para ella si lo descubriera, sin encontrar la llave de su escritorio o la dirección de este cuarto alquilado.... *Las mujeres caníbales del Orinoco*, la más excitante aventura nacida de la pluma de F. Blatsky, dice un anuncio publicado en una de esas revistas que hay tal vez en la sala de espera del detective Blázquez. No, de Black Blake, *piensa sentado ante la máquina*... (196–97; emphases added)

Because Blatsky's imaginary detective is depicted as imagining his own creator, "Borrador de una historia" self-consciously demonstrates an author's ability to invent characters who appear to live independently of their author, as Unamuno did in *Niebla*. After Blatsky imagines a woman arriving at Blázquez's office, he looks up and notices a woman about to enter his office. The story ends by deliberately equating fiction and reality, an effect which has been prepared by the alliterative identification of *Bla*tsky and *Bláz*quez as narrative doubles.

The double—a characteristically self-reflexive strategy—is exploited in both *Beatus ille* and *Beltenebros*. In the latter novel, there are constant references to doubles and mirrors, and even the use of invented names suggests a linguistic preoccupation with self-reflection—the name *Boite Tabú* contains its own phonetic reflection (bu-at/ta-bu).[16] Rebeca Osorio shares her mother's name and is also her identical twin, while the names *Be*ltenebros and *Be*rnal identify two political bosses who resemble each other in that each directs his underlings as if they were pawns in a chess game: "es posible que [Bernal] sólo concediera a la realidad una importancia secundaria: tenía un ensimismamiento de jugador de ajedrez..." (*Beltenebros* 51). However, the most important pair of doubles is that of Darman and Andrade, whose names are near anagrams of each other. Darman says that Andrade "sabía disparar tan certeramente como yo mismo" (10), and when shown the latter's photograph says "Yo era exactamente igual que ese hombre de la fotografía..." (54).

Doubles and mirrors are used in *Beltenebros* to accentuate the fictive nature of the text's referents, for mirror images emphasize the unreality of a two-dimensional simulacrum. In Darman's hotel, the mirrors that reflect plastic trees ("espejos que duplicaban palmeras de plástico" [23]) take unreality one step further, given that reflections of copies are doubly fictive. In addition to mirror images there are several references to mannequins (11, 40, 73) which again allude to the characters' fictional condition of imitations. Darman and Andrade are represented as doubles because they are both demythicized—Darman is not the virtuously heroic resistance member that Luque thinks he is, and neither is Andrade the malicious traitor whom Bernal designates for elimination. Andrade's only "crime" is to have fallen in love with Rebeca, and he is unwittingly drawn into Beltenebros's sphere of influence because of his devotion to her.

In *Beatus ille*, Minaya arrives at his uncle's home and soon enters into an amorous relationship with one of Manuel's assistants, Inés. After Manuel sees the two of them making love, he dies of a fatal heart attack brought on by the memory of Solana, who had been seen by Doña Elvira making love to Manuel's fiancée, Mariana. At one point, the similarity between the two pairs of lovers is deliberately foregrounded by an abrupt and unanticipated change of scene, from Minaya and Inés embracing in Manuel's living room to Solana and Mariana as they make love in Manuel's garden thirty-two years earlier:[17]

> Dijo luego Inés que cuando iba a levantarse para encender la luz Minaya la retuvo a su lado. Quería detener el tiempo, no para dar un paso más allá del instante en que la oscuridad aún los cobijaba como un ala de seda, no volver a la luz usual que lo igualaba todo y los regresaría al pudor, otra vez desconocidos, las manos apresurándose a ordenar la ropa y a borrar de la biblioteca las señales que a la mañana siguiente pudieran descubrirlos.

> Una copa de vino volcada en el césped, una botella vacía, un rectángulo de luz avanzando sin misericordia sobre la penumbra del jardín como un río de cuya crecida se apartaran los amantes sin deshacer el abrazo. Mariana, incorporándose, apoyó su hermosa cabeza... (86)

The juxtaposition identifies Solana as Minaya's double, and this is reinforced when Solana describes Minaya in the same terms he uses later to describe himself:

> Ya no es preciso escribir para adivinar o inventar las cosas. El, Minaya, lo ignora, y supongo que alguna vez se rendirá inevitablemente a la superstición de la escritura... (8)

> [H]e acudido tenazmente a las supersticiones de la literatura y de la memoria para fingir que existía en los actos de aquella noche un orden necesario. (193)

The old man who tells Minaya of Solana's return to Mágina also suggests a similarity between the two: "Me parece que lo [Solana] estoy viendo como lo veo a usted..." (60). The portrayal of Solana and Minaya as doubles is made most explicit at the conclusion of the novel when Solana, the narrator, tells Minaya "Usted ha escrito el libro" (278).

Solana's depiction as Minaya's double underscores that both are author-figures: Solana has wanted to write a book entitled *Beatus ille* and Minaya pretends to be writing a doctoral thesis on the life of Solana, although neither accomplish their professed goals. However, when Solana calls Minaya his "cómplice" (276)—an allusion to Cortázar's description in *Rayuela* of the active reader ("hacer del lector un cómplice" [448])—he identifies Minaya not only as an author but also as a reader.[18] In this way, Solana's imminent death is a reminder of Barthes's dictum that "the birth of the reader must be at the cost of the death of the Author" ("Death" 148): Solana the author lies dying in Mágina as Minaya the reader returns to Madrid.

Notes

1. See Labanyi (35–53).
2. Herzberger defines the novel of memory as "those fictions that evoke past time through subjective remembering, most often through first-person narration" ("Narrating the Past" 35).
3. Like Wayne Booth in *The Rhetoric of Fiction* (70–77), I use the term "implied author" to refer to the mask of the real author, a theoretical construct which controls the ethical norms implicit in a work of fiction.
4. See the poem "Valdivia (1544)" in *Canto general* (172–75).
5. The reference is to *Radio Pirenaica*, which the Spanish Communist Party in exile used to broadcast news to Spain.
6. Muñoz Molina's attempt to go beyond the offical accounts of the Civil War and present history from the standpoint of its participants has a striking parallel in *Luna de lobos* (1985), a novel by Julio Llamazares (b. 1954). Just as Muñoz Molina takes a critical look at Solana and Darman, Llamazares contrasts the townspeople's heroic vision of Angel, a Republican resistance fighter, with Angel's own description of himself. Like Solana, the popular vision of Angel is that of a hero who is "valiente, astuto, inteligente, invencible" (*Luna de lobos* 136). However, Angel realizes that he is simply "[u]n hombre perseguido y solitario. Un hombre acorralado por el miedo y la venganza, por el hambre y el frío" (136).
7. The epigraph to *Beltenebros* is taken from *Don Quijote*, and Darman's comment is no doubt another Cervantine allusion.
8. John Barth's "The Literature of Exhaustion" in *The Atlantic Monthly* August (1967): 29–34 and Robert Scholes' "Metafiction" in *Iowa Review* 1.4 [1970]: 100–115.
9. Patricia Waugh's definition of metafiction paraphrases Alter's: "*Metafiction* is a term given to fictional writing which self-consciously and systematically draws attention to its status as an artefact in order to pose questions about the relationship between fiction and reality" (*Metafiction* 2).
10. For Hutcheon, diegetically self-aware texts are those that are "conscious of their own narrative processes" (*Narcissistic* 23).
11. Like Tzvetan Todorov, I use the term "verisimilitude" "in its most naive sense—'consistent with reality'" ("Introduction" 82).

12 Manuel tells Minaya that "Miguel Hernández...era más joven que nosotros y [Solana] veía en él como un espejo de su propia vida" (*Beatus ille* 31).

13 Similarly, the first-person narrator of *Los misterios de Madrid* remains anonymous until in the final chapter he reveals himself as a character in the story. However, unlike Solana in *Beatus ille*, the pharmacy employee does not violate fictional boundaries, for he limits himself to recounting the story he has been told by Lorencito Quesada.

14 Unlike Bértolo and Azancot, *El País*'s critic Rafael Conte appears to understand metafiction, describing *Beltenebros* as a text "anclado esta vez en la técnica de las novelas de espionaje y conspiraciones políticas, aunque desprovistas de toda suerte de intencionalidad realista" ("*El jinete polaco*" 7).

15 Although never named, the organization is obviously the Spanish Communist Party in exile, the members of which were organizing the resistance in Spain.

16 Other phonetic reflections occur in the names of doubles. As well as *Bl*atsky/*Bl*ázquez, there are *Wa*lter/*Va*ldivia (*Beltenebros*), and Ataúlfo *Ram*iro Reta*mar*/*Ram*ón Tovarich (*El dueño del secreto*).

17 The names of these two pairs of doubles offer another example of phonetic mirrors: M*in*aya-*In*és/Sol*ana*-M*aria*na.

18 "[U]no de los dos cómplices de la literatura es el lector" (Muñoz Molina, "Cuando Onetti").

CHAPTER THREE

Engaging the Reader

> la médula misma de la novela es el acto de leer. ("Desocupado lector")

During the 1960s, literary criticism was predominantly text-centered, informed by the linguistic theories of Ramon Jakobson and the structuralism of Claude Lévi-Strauss.[1] European formalists and Anglo-American New Critics shared a belief in the literary text as an autonomous structure of meaning, and essays like "The Intentional Fallacy" and "The Affective Fallacy" proposed that the intentions of authors and the responses of readers were of little or no importance to interpretation.[2] Even critics like Northrop Frye who claimed to be breaking with the New Criticism continued to stress the autonomy of the text. Elizabeth Freund writes that Frye's system

> constitutes an end in itself *without reference to readers* or contexts of communication. An essentially similar attitude to the function of literary language underlies the poetics of Roman Jakobson... (74; emphasis added).

In contrast to the structuralist's conception of the self-contained text, new critical theories arose which took into account readers' reactions as a crucial element in textual analysis.[3] Although there are varying approaches to what Susan Suleiman calls "audience-oriented criticism," one of the most relevant for the study of Muñoz Molina's work is that of Wolfgang Iser. In an early article, the latter stated that "a text can only come to life when it is read" ("Indeterminacy" 2), a claim similar to one made by Muñoz Molina: "Sin el lector no existe el libro" (Azancot, Nuria n. pag.).

Like Iser and other audience-oriented critics, Muñoz Molina has consistently pointed out in his articles that literature is inconceivable without the reader. In "Desocupado lector," he writes that "[e]l lector es el gran continente ignorado de la literatura.... [L]a médula misma de la novela es el acto de leer," and in "Novela de una novela," he affirms that "la literatura no existe sin la resonancia del lector" (23). It is evident that his theoretical commentaries reflect his novelistic practice, for all of his texts use specific strategies to engage the reader's active participation and make him/her, in Roland Barthes's words, "no longer a consumer, but a producer of the text" (*S/Z* 4).

In *The Act of Reading*, Wolfgang Iser proposes that the meaning of a text be treated not as an object to be identified but as an effect to be experienced by the reader. The meaning of a text is a process rather than a product, and elements of indeterminacy oblige the reader to extract potential meanings through acts of "concretization" (*Act* 21), "actualization" (24), or "realization" (69):

> it is the elements of indeterminacy that enable the text to 'communicate' with the reader, in the sense that they induce him to participate both in the production and the comprehension of the work's intention.... [T]he relative indeterminacy of a text allows a spectrum of actualizations. (*Act* 24)

Iser writes of "*relative* indeterminacy," for although he believes that individual readings will produce a variety of different actualizations, it is ultimately "the limits imposed by the written as opposed to the unwritten text" (*Implied* [282]) that control the parameters of interpretation.[4] The realization of a text is therefore a cooperative enterprise which depends on both the author's text and the reader's imagination in actualizing it: "author and reader are to share the game of the imagination" (*Act* 108).

The concept of indeterminacy or "gaps" is basic to Iser's theory, for only indeterminacy allows the reader's active participation in actualizing the text:

> there must be a place within this [textual] system for the person who is to perform the reconstituting. This place is marked by the gaps in the text— it consists in the blanks which the reader is to fill in.... The gaps function as a kind of pivot on which the whole text-reader relationship revolves. Hence the structured blanks of the text stimulate the process of ideation to be performed by the reader on terms set by the text. (*Act* 169)

Iser's description of "gaps" and "structured blanks" are analogous to Muñoz Molina's description of the blank spaces ("espacios en blanco") of *El invierno en Lisboa*, a novel in which he aimed to engage the reader's imagination by deliberately exploiting textual indeterminacy:

> *En Beatus ille* había querido contarlo todo: antes de comenzar *El invierno en Lisboa* me di cuenta de que era preferible decir lo menos posible, rodear las palabras escritas de grandes espacios en blanco para que la historia sugerida se estableciese con más plenitud en la imaginación del lector. ("El secreto de Santiago Biralbo" 109)

> Dejo esos espacios en blanco para que el lector los complete. Creo que una parte del proceso de aprendizaje del escritor es saber callar a tiempo, saber no decir las cosas, porque las cosas que no se dicen tienen más fuerza que las cosas que se dicen. (Martín Gil 28)

El invierno en Lisboa illustrates Iser's concept of the need for the "ideational" or imaginative activity of the reader to fill in areas of indeterminacy, particularly in the case of the novel's narrator. The text gives almost no information about him—he lacks a name, he is never physically described, his profession is unknown, and almost nothing is said of his past. With this absence of data, the reader is obliged to create his/her own image of the narrator, including his physical appearance. This recalls Iser's comment that unlike the visible protagonist in a film, "the hero in the novel must be pictured and cannot be seen. With the novel the reader must use his imagination to synthesize the information given him" (*Implied* 283).

In *Narrative Fiction*, Shlomith Rimmon-Kenan discusses the process of reading, noting that a text

> must make certain that it will be read; its very existence, as it were, depends on it. Interestingly, the text is caught here in a double bind. On the one hand, in order to be read it must make itself understood, it must enhance intelligibility.... But if the text is understood too quickly, it would thereby come to an untimely end. So, on the other hand, it is in the text's interest to slow down the process of comprehension by the reader so as to ensure its own survival. (122–3)

Because a text's existence "depends on maintaining the phase of the 'not yet fully known or intelligible' for as long as possible" (125), authors will often delay imparting vital information. Such delays

> can create suspense of two different types: future-oriented and past-oriented.... The future-oriented type consists in keeping alive the question 'what next?' (and is thus related to Barthes's proairetic code).... The past-oriented delay consist in keeping alive questions like 'what happened?' 'who did it?', 'why?'... (125–126)

David Lodge provides a similar analysis, adding that the second type of delay corresponds to Barthes's hermeneutic code, the effect of which produces "mystery" rather than "suspense:"

> [Narrative] obtains and holds the interest of its audience by raising questions in their minds about the process it describes, and delaying the answers to those questions, or raising new questions... The questions are basically of two kinds: what happens next? which generates suspense; and what happened in the past, and why? which generates mystery. (Roland Barthes calls them the proairetic and hermeneutic codes, respectively.) (*After Bakhtin* 146)

Several examples will illustrate how Muñoz Molina uses the technique of delayed information in both his fiction and non-fiction. "Los manteQueros de Perú," a newspaper article, begins with a conjectural description of what appears to be a series of kidnappings:

> Para actuar con eficacia seguramente elegían la noche y los caminos despoblados, y es posible que no lo hicieran al azar, apostándose al anochecher en una encrucijada, esperando sin más que pasara algún caminante desprevenido y solitario. Escogerían con preferencia a personas jóvenes y bien entradas en carnes y las seguirían en secreto.... Los más gordos no sólo eran los más adecuados por la favorable proporción entre gananacia y esfuerzo, sino también porque solían ser de carácter bovino y poco belicoso...

This first paragraph—which occupies one third of the entire article—gives no explanation for these mysterious kidnappings, nor does it reveal who is committing them. Neither does the reader know whether the account is reality or fiction. The paragraph concludes:

> Circulaban rumores alentados por el miedo, pero parecían más bien residuos de antiguas fábulas inventadas para asustar a los niños. Hay cosas que es preferible no creer, y espantos que han de ser atribuidos a la irresponsabilidad de la literatura o a la de los sueños.

The final two sentences create both suspense and mystery by suggesting that the truth is so horrifying as to border on the fantastic. The title offers a small clue, but not until the second paragraph is the delayed information given:

> Eran dos hombres muy jóvenes, de 22 y 19 años, y cuando la policía los detuvo, hará unas tres semanas, confesaron que no trabajaban por su cuenta, sino por encargo de un hombre que vivía en la capital.... Desde la capital, el intermediario la remitía [la grasa de los cuerpos] a Estados Unidos, donde una firma de cosméticos la empleaba como materia prima en la elaboración de cremas hidratantes.

This technique of withholding information is used in a similar manner in "El regreso de Lázaro," another newspaper article which begins:

> No saben dónde han estado: tan sólo que habrían querido no volver, que pasarán el resto de sus vidas imaginando la repetición de un viaje que la próxima vez ya será definitivo...

Throughout the entire first paragraph, the reader is told of a "journey" which certain unidentified people have taken, but the destination is unclear. The only hints given are the article's title and a reference to the subjects coming from a hospital ("Vienen del hospital"). The first paragraph concludes enigmatically: "su viaje los llevó al otro lado de la oscuridad y el terror y las palabras son inútiles para contar lo que nadie más que uno ha visto." As in "Los mantequeros," indeterminacy generates suspense and mystery, after which all is abruptly clarified in the first sentence of the second paragraph: "Son hombres y mujeres que han regresado de la proximidad o de las primeras galerías de la muerte." The "viaje" and "el otro lado" have been used as metaphors for death, and the reader realizes retroactively that the first paragraph alludes to those people who have survived death and near-death experiences.

In the two articles just mentioned, Muñoz Molina withholds information in order to engage the interest of his readers, who must continue beyond the first paragraph in order to dispel an enigma created by textual indeterminacy. In "Un amor imposible" (*Nada del otro mundo*), the author goes even further and waits until the very end of the story to clarify the events recounted. The text begins with the description of a man and a woman preparing for a sexual encounter:

> Cuando empieza a sonar muy despacio la música y ella tiende los brazos llamándome yo hago siempre como si no me enterara...ella...arrodillada, abrazándome la cintura, irguiéndose lentamente desde el suelo, como sedienta, pero es mentira y yo lo sé, ni siquiera me mira a los ojos... (185)

The setting for this encounter is described as a room with a light and a red carpet, possibly in an apartment building, since the narrator mentions "el bar de abajo" (186). The narrator's visits are described as routine, and the woman's indifference to him suggests that he might be visiting a prostitute. Not until the final sentence does the reader realize that the narrator is a performer in a sex show:

> cuando se enciendan las luces de la sala y suenen los aplausos de esas gentes sombrías que nos están mirando, ella saldrá por las cortinas rojas y será otra vez una desconocida que después de ducharse se viste como se quitara un uniforme al terminar su trabajo. (189)

It should be noted that even in the final sentence there is a hint of indeterminacy—the sex show is never explicitly referred to although it is inferred from the fact that people are watching and applauding.

Another of the author's preferred techniques is that of foreshadowing future scenes with unexplained and uncontextualized references to characters who have not yet appeared physically in the text, an example of Barthes's hermeneutic code (*S/Z* 17). At the beginning of *Beatus ille*, Solana narrates:

> donde tal vez guarde el olvido varios rostros no exactamente iguales de Mariana, la estampa de Manuel cuando subió tras ella con su uniforme de teniente, la expresión que tuvieron por única vez los ojos de Jacinto Solana en la madrugada del 21 de mayo de 1937, víspera ignorada del crimen... (14)

This passage is highly disconcerting, because neither Solana nor Mariana have yet entered the story, and the reader has no idea who they are nor what their future roles in the story will be. The reference to a "crime" is also unexplained, for not until chapter 3 does the reader discover that Mariana had been shot. Similarly, the opening of *El jinete polaco* introduces characters whom the reader will not encounter until much further on in the text. Manuel and Nadia are described as

> vinculados...por la figura del jinete que cabalga a través de un paisaje nocturno, por las pupilas fijas...de una mujer emparedada que permaneció incorrupta durante setenta años, por el baúl de las fotografías de Ramiro Retratista y una Biblia protestante... (10)

Neither the mummy nor Ramiro have yet been presented, and the reader is left to guess at their possible significance for Manuel and Nadia. In both of the passages just cited, Muñoz Molina creates an enigmatic textual gap, a deliberate delaying tactic to leave the reader anticipating future events.

One technique which uses delayed information is what Iser calls "cutting" (*Act* 191–2). Nineteenth-century authors of serial novels would purposely end each installment by breaking off the story at a point where the reader is anxious to know the outcome of a situation:

> The interruption and consequent prolongation of tension is the basic function of the cut. The result is that we try to imagine how the story will unfold, and in this way we heighten our own participation in the course of events. Dickens was a master of the technique; his readers became his 'co-authors'. (*Act* 191)[5]

It is not surprising that Muñoz Molina, an author who deliberately aims at engaging his readers' interest, has written a parody of the Spanish *novela de entregas* in which he makes ample use of cutting and hermeneutic gaps to generate suspense. *Los misterios de Madrid*, his fifth novel, was originally published in installments in the newspaper *El País*, each of the twenty-eight chapters appearing daily over the course of four weeks.[6] Although it was later published as a novel, its original newspaper version was most probably a calculated consumer-oriented strategy to keep readers buying the newspaper in order to follow the story, as in the case of the nineteenth-century *novelas de entregas*.

Los misterios opens as the protagonist, Lorencito Quesada, unexpectedly receives a telephone call from an important local aristocrat, don Sebastián Guadalimar, who urgently wishes to talk with him. The titles of both the novel[7] and of the first chapter—"Una cita enigmática"—recall Barthes's hermeneutic code, and the narrator self-consciously emphasizes this when he says "le faltaba una hora de duración intolerable para acudir a aquella cita que él ya había calificado de enigmática" (11). When Quesada meets don Sebastián, the latter is visibly distraught and begs for help. The first chapter concludes with the reason for the call:

> —Nos han robado, amigo mío—dijo, con la voz sorda y rota, como de no haber dormido en muchas noches—. Nos han robado la imagen del Santo Cristo de la Greña. (12)

The end of the first chapter both answers a question (Why has don Sebastián called Quesada?) and asks another (Who robbed the processional figure?). Suspense is generated in a similar manner throughout the novel as each chapter abruptly terminates with the introduction of new characters (chapter 2),[8] the anticipation of future adventures (chapter 3), and the mysterious interruption of telephone calls (chapters 4 and 5).

Iser remarks that the cutting technique depends on the text's presentation in serial form:

> The serial story, then, results in a special kind of reading.... The reader is forced by the pauses imposed on him to imagine more than he could have if his readings were continuous, and so, if the text of a serial makes a different impression from the text in book-form, this is principally because it introduces additional blanks, or alternatively accentuates existing blanks by means of a break until the next installment. This does not mean that its quality is in any way higher. (*Act* 192)

Iser's discussion is extremely pertinent to *Los misterios de Madrid*, for it raises the question of whether or not cutting as a means of generating suspense was nullified by subsequently publishing the story as a single volume. I shall leave this question—as Muñoz Molina no doubt would—for his readers to decide.

Muñoz Molina's use of cutting is characteristic of *El invierno en Lisboa* and *Beltenebros*, both of which use the conclusions of chapters to maintain suspense and thus engage the reader. The first chapter of *El invierno en Lisboa* ends as the narrator takes leave of Santiago Biralbo:

> Cuando lo vi volver...entendí que había en él esa intensa sugestión de carácter que tienen siempre los portadores de una historia, como los portadores de un revólver. Pero no estoy haciendo una vana comparación literaria: él tenía una historia y guardaba un revólver. (15)

The final sentence presents two enigmas: What is Santiago's story? and Why is a jazz musician carrying a gun? The second chapter ends as the narrator opens Lucrecia's last letter to Santiago, only to find "un sobre vacío" (22), a self-conscious metaphor for another hermeneutic gap. Other chapters conclude in a similar manner, opening new possibilities and presenting further enigmas.

The endings of chapters in *Beltenebros* also open hermeneutic gaps. The first chapter ends as Darman describes being picked up by a taxi driver outside the airport of Florence:

> "Señor", oí que me decían, "¿esperaba usted un taxi?". Dije que sí, me acomodé en el interior frotándome las manos, y antes de que se me ocurriera decidir dónde iría comprendí que el idioma inusual y sonoro que hablaba el conductor era el duro español de mi adolescencia. (19)

In this particular instance, the cutting opens an enigma for which the reader can imagine at least two possible explanations. If an Italian taxi-driver speaks Spanish, he is probably not a taxi-driver but a Spanish agent sent to pick up Darman (which in fact proves to be the case). However, because Darman is not picked up at the appointed time, suspicion is raised that the taxi-driver might also be a Francoist spy sent to kidnap and/or eliminate Darman. The reader can not know with certainty which of these two options is the correct one. Ending the chapter abruptly at this point produces suspense and anticipation and impels the reader to continue to the next chapter.

Muñoz Molina has always been a devotee of detective fiction, and this is reflected in his fiction.[9] One of his earliest published works is a detective story entitled "Te golpearé sin cólera," and the protagonist Walberg of

"La gentileza de los desconocidos" (*Nada del otro mundo*) acts as an amateur detective by using his keen sense of observation and acute intelligence to discover that his friend, Quintana, is a murderer.[10] Other characters portrayed as amateur detectives are Minaya (who in *Beatus ille* discovers the identity of Mariana's murder), Manuel (who in *El jinete polaco* solves the mystery of the mummy) and Lorencito Quesada (who in *Los misterios de Madrid* finds the stolen processional image).

Perhaps the major reason for Muñoz Molina's interest in detective fiction is his belief that our lives are dominated by the need to understand the world, a yearning to *know* which is a primary trait of the detective and one which many of Muñoz Molina's characters share. Minaya is characterized by "[el] deseo y...la voluntad de saber" (*Beatus ille* 37), "el insomne deseo de conocimiento" (262) and "su voluntad de saber" (276). Biralbo is "un adolescente fortalecido por el conocimiento" (*El invierno en Lisboa* 10) whose eyes show "el brillo del coraje y del conocimiento" (14). On seeing Andrade's photo, Darman is "inmediatamente poseído por el deseo de saber" (*Beltenebros* 52), and when he interrogates Rebeca Osorio, he says "yo tenía que saber" (165). In "La edad de la novela," Muñoz Molina attributes this desire for knowledge to authors and readers alike: "Quien escribe no lo hace sólo para contar: lo hace para saber, y en eso se parece al lector." In *La realidad de la ficción*, he writes "Conocer es un trabajo, pues, de detective y de novelista" (32).

Historically there are two different strains of detective fiction: the "classical" or "formal" detective novel and the "hard-boiled" crime thriller.[11] Each has attained great popularity because mystery and suspense are fundamental strategies in engaging reader participation. Consequently, Muñoz Molina draws freely from both models, using delayed information to raise questions about what *will* happen (the proairetic code) and also what *has* happened (the hermeneutic code). I will now turn to Muñoz Molina's adaptation of the classical detective story or "whodunit," a genre that elicits the reader's participation not only in anticipating future events but in discovering the truth about past ones.

The detective story was until recently disparaged as failing to meet the requirements of "serious" literature.[12] Nevertheless, there is now a vast number of critical studies of this genre, many of which discuss the detective story's self-conscious foregrounding of its narrative structure. Linda Hutcheon calls it a "very self-conscious" form (*Narcissistic* 31), and S. E. Sweeney writes that "all detective stories refer, if only obliquely, to their own fictionality and their own interpretation," noting that "detective fiction...represents narrativity in its purest form" (3).

In addition to its self-reflexiveness, the detective story depends for its full effect on the reader, who aligned with the detective participates in a hermeneutic endeavor: understanding how and why a crime has been committed. George Grella notes that the discovery of the circumstances surrounding a mysterious event "could describe a number of literary works, including *Oedipus Rex, Hamlet, Tom Jones,* and *Absalom, Absalom!*" ("Murder" 37). George Dove states that while the hermeneutic is present in all fiction, "in the detective story it defines the genre and *dominates the purpose of reading*" (30; emphasis added), while S. E. Sweeney points out that "the detective story reflects reading itself" (7). Given that the detective story both foregrounds narrativity and reflects the reading process itself, it is a highly appropriate model for Muñoz Molina, illustrating both his fascination with metafictional writing and his concern for the role of the reader.

The classical or "formal" detective story is by nature self-reflexive in that it contains two stories: that of the crime and that of the detective's investigation. Tzvetan Todorov notes that these two stories correspond to the narratological distinction between story and discourse:

> We might further characterize these two stories by saying that the first—the story of the crime—tells "what really happened," whereas the second—the story of the investigation—explains "how the reader (or the narrator) has come to know about it." But these definitions concern not only the two stories in detective fiction, but also two aspects of every literary work which the Russian Formalists isolated forty years ago. They distinguished, in fact, the *fable* (story) from the *subject* (plot) of a narrative: the story is what has happened in life, the plot is the way the author presents it to us. ("Typology" 45; author's emphases)

True to his formalist orientation, Todorov virtually ignores the role of the reader in this essay aside from his cursory reference to "how the reader (or the narrator) has come to know about it." Nevertheless, reader-response is of the utmost importance for the detective story's effect, because a full appreciation of the form depends not only on the reader's acceptance of the convention but also on his/her identification with the detective as someone who seeks the answer to an enigma.

In his search for the criminal, the detective acts as a "reader" who must construct a narrative version of the crime from a number of clues in an indecipherable "text." According to Peter Hühn:

> The initial crime—as long as it remains unsolved—functions as an uninterpretable sign.... The progress of the plot (that is, the second story) is then presented as a succession of attempts to ascribe meaning to the sign by finding the missing links to the accepted patterns of reality.... The attempt to read the mystery in this way presupposes the existence of a *text*. (453–4; author's emphasis)

For Hühn, the clues that the detective finds form a metaphorical text which must be "read" by the detective. The difficulty of this reading process lies in

> the criminal's attempts to prevent the detective from deciphering the true meaning of his text. This is basically a contest between an author and a reader about the possession of meaning, each of them wishing to secure it for himself. (The contest *within* the novel is repeated on a higher level between the novelist and the actual reader). (456; author's emphasis)

Hühn perceptively notes that the self-reflexiveness of the detective novel lies in its duplication of the author-reader struggle. *Within* the text, the criminal (as author) attempts to evade the detective (as reader). *Outside* the text, the struggle is that of an extratextual author with his/her readers, for the latter's interest can only be maintained by denying them the solution to the crime until the final pages. Rimmon-Kenan stresses that "if the text is understood too quickly, it would thereby come to an untimely end" (122–3), and this is evidently the case of the detective novel, in which an unduly anticipated revelation of the criminal's identity and of the motive for the crime would abort the narrative.

Beatus ille is a novel that incorporates the hermeneutic enterprise of the detective novel, but modifies the conventions of the genre by doing so. Like the detective novel, it presents an unsolved crime: the murder of Mariana who was shot in 1937 on the roof of Manuel's home. Minaya acts as a detective would in discovering the criminal, Utrera, by "reading" the clues he finds: a bullet, the manure stains on Mariana's skirt, a letter incriminating Utrera. Although Minaya is not a professional detective, his role as one is self-consciously foregrounded as he prepares to reveal the solution:

> [Minaya] llevaba en un bosillo la carta...como esos detectives de los libros que reúnen en el salón a los habitantes de una casa cerrada donde se cometió un crimen para revelarles el nombre del asesino... (241)

Nevertheless, *Beatus ille* is not a conventional detective novel because the story of Mariana's murder is only a sub-plot within a larger story, that of the life and writings of the Civil War poet Solana. Minaya does not come to Mágina to discover Mariana's murderer but because he has been shown Solana's poems by Luque, giving him a pretext to escape the repressive political climate of Madrid and return to what he hopes will be the peaceful life of the countryside. He tells his uncle he has come to write a doctoral thesis on Solana, but initially he has no intention of investigating the poet's life. A combination of guilt—he is penniless and taking advantage of his uncle's hospitality—and curiosity eventually draw him into the investigation, during which he also discovers that Mariana was murdered.

Mariana's murder is resolved in a manner typical of the classical detective novel, as Minaya closes information gaps by "reading" the clues he finds. However, there is a surprise revelation that follows his unmasking of Utrera: he learns that Solana is not dead and has been the narrator of *Beatus ille*. The narrator's anonymity is an information gap of which the reader only becomes aware in retrospect, a phenomenon described by Rimmon-Kenan:

> The reader may or may not have been aware of the existence of a gap in the process of reading. When he is, the gap is *prospective*, and the reading process becomes (at least partly) an attempt to fill it in. But sometimes a text can prevent the reader from asking the right question until it is answered. The gap, in this case, is *retrospective*.... Only after the fact does the reader realize that some significant information has been withheld from him. (129)

Because s/he assumes that Solana is dead, the reader does not realize that the latter is in fact the narrator until the end of the novel. In this way, the reader's attention is retroactively directed to another "crime," that of the narrator's deliberate deception of his readers. *Beatus ille* may therefore be viewed as a double-layered detective novel with *two* crimes instead of one: a crime of murder which has occurred on the diegetic level of the story, and a crime of literary deception on the level of the narration.

Although there are two enigmas in *Beatus ille*—Who killed Mariana? and Who is the narrator?—the reader is seduced into focusing on the diegetic world of the story and the mystery of Mariana's death through Muñoz Molina's strategy of having the first-person "I" continually disappear behind an omniscient third-person narrator. Because the presence of the latter is a traditional guarantee of verisimilitude and of the narrator's authority, the reader is lead to accept Solana's death just as the characters do. If Solana is assumed to be dead, the reader has little reason to question the narrator's identity, for the text "can prevent the reader from asking the right question" (Rimmon-Kenan 129).

The criminal's attempt to elude the detective is "a contest between an author and a reader" (Hühn 456), which is to say that the author (as criminal) must constantly try to throw the reader (as detective) off the hermeneutic path. Muñoz Molina does this by convincing the reader that Solana is dead, but he does not forget the detective author's traditional obligation to provide the reader with clues which theoretically could be used to deduce the narrator's identity. Unlike the traditional detective plot, in which physical objects provide part of the evidence (as in the case of Mariana), the clues to Solana's identity are primarily discursive phenomena, and a retroactive reading of *Beatus ille* reveals them scattered throughout the text. "[P]uedo, si quiero, imaginarlo todo para mí solo, es decir, *para nadie*," says the anonymous narrator in Chapter 1 (7; emphasis added). Four chapters later, Minaya discovers an inscription by Solana which reads: "Quién hubiera tenido el coraje de ser el capitán Nemo. Mi nombre es nadie, dice Ulises..." (52). The narrator also says "Ya *no es preciso escribir* para adivinar o inventar las cosas" and refers to "*el valor del silencio*" (8; emphases added). Ten pages later Minaya reads Solana's poem in which "las palabras sona[b]an...con un sereno propósito de perfección y silencio, como si...no importara...el acto de escribir" (18). The description of Solana's diary carries one of the most explicit clues, a description of the narrative technique of *Beatus Ille*:

> A veces Solana escribía en primera persona, y otras veces usaba la tercera como si quisiera ocultar la voz que lo contaba y lo adivinaba todo, para dar así a la narración el tono de una crónica impasible. (89)

In the case of Mariana's murder, the reader does not have access to the most important clue—the incriminating letter to Utrera—until Minaya explains his solution of the crime. Nevertheless, Muñoz Molina does provide a clue based on a convention of the detective story, that of the "Most Likely Suspect" (Dove 32). By portraying Utrera and Doña Elvira as "especially despicable or loathsome" (32), the reader is warned of their possible implication in Mariana's death. Another clue—based on Muñoz Molina's penchant for names and anagrams—points to Utrera as Mariana's murderer.[13] When Medina is talking about the spy who was lynched by the townspeople of Mágina, he says "sus últimas palabras fueron un nombre,

Victor o tal vez Héctor Vera, o Vega" (175). Previously, Utrera's name has been described appearing on statues in Roman letters as *VTRERA* (39; emphasis added). The association of the two names covertly anticipates that Utrera was Victor Vega's contact. Nevertheless, given that the author prevents the reader from solving the crime before Minaya does, these clues may only be appreciated by a retroactive reading.

Inscribing the reader

One of the most paradoxical aspects of fiction is that the reader must temporarily accept a textual world as if it were real—with a "willing suspension of disbelief"—while simultaneously realizing that it is only a fiction. Authors of metafiction often foreground this phenomenon by using characters to mirror the reading process itself, and the detective—as we have seen—acts as an inscribed reader of the story of a crime. Given that Muñoz Molina's characters often resort to their imagination and memory to form narrative versions of both past and present events, I would now propose that in doing so they function implicitly or explicitly as inscribed readers, "reading" the fictional worlds they inhabit as if they were texts and actualizing the gaps and indeterminacies confronting them.[14]

Marino in "La poseída" (*Nada del otro mundo*) is, like a real reader, faced with an enigmatic "text"—the girl in the bar. Because he never speaks to her, can only see her for brief periods, and knows nothing of her past, he must "concretize" her story as if he were reading an enigmatic text replete with gaps. The story is focalized exclusively through the eyes of Marino so that the extratextual reader, limited to Marino's point of view, is just as surprised as the latter is when he finds that the girl is not suffering from love-sickness but from drug addiction. Marino is therefore depicted as an inscribed reader, but an incompetent one guilty of *mis*reading. It should be noted that although "La poseída" is not a detective story, its title is also a clue for the extratextual reader, one which can only be understood retroactively: the girl is "possessed" not by love, but by her drug habit.[15]

Marino's misreading of the girl is understandable given the communicative—or rather non-communicative—context in which he finds himself. If he had spoken with the girl, he would no doubt have realized she was a drug addict, for oral communication offers the possibility of mutual exchange in which both parties may respond to, revise and correct the content of a verbal message. However, as an inscribed reader Marino is confronted with what is a "silent" text, the gaps of which he fails to fill in correctly until he sees the girl's body lying on the restroom floor. Similarly, Santiago in "El hombre sombra" (*Nada del otro mundo*) never communicates directly with Nélida, for although he can hear her voice over the telephone, he can neither speak to her nor see her. Both Marino and Santiago are therefore limited to being the receivers of what they initially perceive as indecipherable texts which neither can interpret successfully. While Marino is incompetent and falls into misreading, Santiago could be called a reluctant reader, for when he finally gets the opportunity to meet Nélida in the park, he flees from her, symbolically rejecting to "read" her any further.

Commenting on the narrator of *El invierno en Lisboa*, Muñoz Molina has said "El lector se ve forzado a construir él mismo el personaje, a inventarlo o incluso convertirse en él" (Solana VII). By suggesting that the real reader must "become" the narrator, the author is pointing out that the narrator is in fact an inscription of the reader. Like the real reader, the narrator is also faced with having to "read" Santiago Biralbo's story, which he concretizes from a metaphorical text made up of letters, newspaper clippings, records, and conversations with the musician and his friends. Relying on his imagination and memory, he creates a coherent narrative from a text riddled with gaps and indeterminacies. When he opens the last of Lucrecia's letters only to find that the envelope is empty, the "sobre vacío" (22) becomes a metaphor for the blank spaces and indeterminacies which a real reader encounters in a text. *El invierno en Lisboa* is a metafictional work that in addition to self-consciously parodying the genre of the popular thriller and its cinematic adaptation in *film noir*, also thematizes the process of reading. As an author, the narrator "writes" Biralbo's story, but he must first "read" it, which he does by supplanting its indeterminacies with his own narrative imagination and memory.

Like the narrator of *El invierno en Lisboa*, Minaya in *Beatus ille* functions as an inscribed reader. He comes to Mágina to discover the story of Solana's past by reading a series of "texts" that include conversations, photographs, and a genuine text—Solana's diary. Like the narrator of *El invierno en Lisboa* who reconstructs the story of Biralbo, Minaya creates his own narrative version of Solana's life, and when the latter tells him "ha sido en su imaginación donde hemos vuelto a nacer" (278), the poet describes Minaya's activity as analogous to that of Iser's reader who has concretized the events of a story with the aid of textual evidence supplemented by his own imagination and memory. Minaya becomes a co-creator of the book which Solana has written, and this is underscored when the latter calls him his "cómplice" (276).¹⁶ By inscribing Solana and Minaya as an author and a reader respectively, Muñoz Molina demonstrates Iser's claim that the aesthetic response is a collaboration between the two poles of a literary work: "the artistic and the esthetic: the artistic refers to the text created by the author, and the esthetic to the realization accomplished by the reader" (*Implied* 274). When Solana tells Minaya "Usted ha escrito el libro" (278), he is referring to Minaya's role as an active reader who by actualizing a text becomes, in effect, its author as well as its reader.

In *Beltenebros*, characters are depicted as explicitly literary creations whose names are taken from the world of fiction—Rebeca is "un nombre del cine" (167),¹⁷ and Andrade's pseudonyms are "nombres en general irreales como de novela" (7). The world in which Darman moves is described as if it were a fictional text, as unreal as the content of Rebeca Osorio's novels. Consequently, Darman can also be seen as an inscribed reader, lost in a textual world that he cannot "read," one in which "arbitrarias columnas" (8) recall Baudelaire's "vivants piliers," which "laissent parfois sortir de confuses paroles" (*Obra* 41). When Darman finds the older Rebeca writing on "una máquina de escribir donde no había ningún papel" (216), the absence of paper—metonymically reinforced by a movie projected without sound—is like Lucrecia's letter emblematic of the "gaps" that Darman has encountered throughout the novel.

In *El jinete polaco*, Manuel offers another case of an inscribed reader confronted with "texts" which include photographs, conversations, memories, letters and don Mercurio's Bible. Manuel "reads" to reconstruct the story of his past, and also plays the role of a detective who, by interrogating Julián, finally solves the mystery of the mummy. When he says "Yo soy...el testigo de mi propia narración" (180), he is referring to his role as an autobiographer who is both the author and reader of his past, "the reader of his own fiction and by implication of his own life" (Hornung 175). He is portrayed, as it were, as his own double.

The use of doubles was mentioned in chapter 2 as a self-reflexive or metafictional strategy used to underscore the fictive nature of the text's characters. Muñoz Molina also uses doubles to emphasizes the parallel and often interchangeable roles of authors and readers, which I have noted in the cases of Minaya and Solana (*Beatus ille*) and Manuel (*El jinete polaco*). In *El Robinson urbano* and "Borrador de una historia" (*Nada del otro mundo*), this doubling phenomenon again underscores the role of characters as inscribed readers.

Urban Robinson is the fictional alter-ego of the narrator-author Muñoz Molina. As a *flâneur*, Robinson walks about Granada and "reads" the city's landscape and inhabitants as if they were texts. John Rignall has noted that the *flâneur* "combines the casual eye of the stroller with the purposeful gaze of the detective" (114), and Robinson may be seen as a combination of *flâneur*, detective, and inscribed reader. At the same time, he is depicted returning to "esa habitación donde lo esperan la máquina y el papel en blanco" (*El Robinson urbano* 107), which identifies him as an author as well as the narrator's double. When the narrator is seen reading a letter which Robinson has left him (135–6), by reading the letter he becomes—like Manuel in *El jinete polaco*—his own narratee, an author reading what his other self has written.

In "Borrador de una historia" (*Nada del otro mundo*), Blatsky is portrayed as a writer of pulp fiction, but is initially described as a reader looking at a newspaper kiosk. In fact, his success as a writer depends on his role as a reader, for his plots are for the most part extracted from news articles, books and sensationalist magazines. Even his idea for a fictional character, Blázquez, comes from reading the latter's name on a plaque in an office building and from his knowledge of detective stories. Blázquez, in turn, is depicted as a reader who has been buying Blatsky's novels. However, both Blatsky and Blázquez are also author-figures who imaginatively construct each other, and the story ends as Blatsky begins writing his "Capítulo primero" (*Nada del otro mundo* 200). Reading and writing are here seen as activities that mirror each other, implying that every reader is also a writer, filling in the indeterminacies of a text by "authoring" what s/he reads.[18]

Real vs. Implied Readers

In this chapter I have drawn on Iser's central thesis that readers "are…forced to take an active part in the composition of [a] novel's meaning" (*Implied* xii). My discussion has been limited to extratextual (real) readers, who must fill in gaps and indeterminacies, and inscribed readers, who as fictional characters serve to mirror the activity of the former. There has been no mention of the term "implied reader," an intentional omission which must be justified.

Iser attempts to distinguish between real and implied readers, but he states that the term "implied reader" "incorporates *both* the prestructuring of the potential meaning by the text, *and* the [real] reader's actualization of this potential through the reading process" (*Implied* xii; emphases added). Elizabeth Freund points out that this confuses the distinction:

> By using this double-barrelled definition, Iser manages to distinguish and divide and at the same time to join 'the reader's role as a textual structure, and the reader's role as a structured act'... The sophistication of this dialectical maneuvering, however, is achieved at the cost of blurring the distinction which Iser assumes throughout his work between the conceptualized phenomenological reader and empirical or historical readers. (144)[19]

To avoid any terminological confusion, I have followed Rimmon-Kenan and Gérard Genette, who identify the implied reader with the extradiegetic narratee, making the former term superfluous and unnecessary.[20] In my opinion, this does not detract from the force of Iser's main argument, which is that texts manifest structures that control the extratextual reader's responses. However, it does leave open up the question of reader *reception*, or how a literary work's frame of reference depends on "a previous understanding of the genre [and] from the forms and themes of already familiar works" (Jauss, "Literary" 15).[21] Consequently, in the following chapter I will discuss the question of Muñoz Molina's work in relation to popular genres and the conventional expectations of his real, historical readers.[22]

Notes

[1] Both Jakobson and Lévi-Strauss collaborated in a linguistic analysis of Baudelaire's "Les Chats," included in Jakobson's *Language in Literature* (180–197). Jonathan Culler provides a summary of structuralist approaches to literature in *Structuralist Poetics*, in which he also critiques Jakobson's poetic analyses (55–74).

[2] See W. K. Wimsatt's *The Verbal Icon*.

[3] An excellent survey of these can be found in Suleiman's introduction to *The Reader in the Text*.

[4] Comparing the invariable components of a text to the stars in the sky, Iser says that just as two observers may see either a dipper or a plough, two readers may also attribute different meanings to a text. "The 'stars' in a literary text are fixed; the lines that join them are variable" (*Implied* 282).

[5] Cervantes uses cutting self-consciously in *Don Quijote* when he abruptly stops recounting the fight between don Quijote and the Basque at the end of Part I, Chapter 8.

[6] The note on page 190 of the original Seix-Barral edition of *Los misterios de Madrid* is incorrect. The first chapter was in fact published on August 12th, 1992, not August 11th.

[7] The novel's title is a parodic intertext. (See Chapter 4, p. 87).

[8] "One common means of intensifying the reader's imaginative activity is suddenly to cut to new characters or even to different plot-lines, so that the reader is forced to try to find connections between the hitherto familiar story and the new, unforeseeable situations" (Iser, *Act* 192).

[9] See his articles "Lectura y adicción," "El detective inexistente" and "Los detectives."

[10] Joaquín Marco, in his review of *Nada del otro mundo*, has said that this story "no sólo utiliza la técnica del cuento policiaco, sino que puede considerarse como tal."

[11] For descriptions of both, see George Grella's articles "Murder and Manners: The Formal Detective Novel" and "The Hard-Boiled Detective Novel."

[12] See Edmund Wilson's essay "Who Cares Who Killed Roger Ackroyd?"

[13] See the discussion of names and doubles in Chapter 2.

14 "Based on the information he receives, every character must construct the facts and the characters around him; thus, he parallels exactly the reader who is constructing the imaginary universe from his own information (the text, and his sense of what is probable); thus, reading becomes (inevitably) one of the themes of the book" (Todorov, "Reading as Construction" 78).

15 Muñoz Molina's titles often provide clues to textual mysteries. The phrase "Beatus ille" is used ironically by Horace in his panegyric of the non-commercial life of the countryside, for the poem is eventually revealed to be narrated by Alfius, a moneylender who has no desire to leave his materialistic city ways. The reader of Horace's poem does not learn the narrator's identity until the end of the text, in the same way that Solana is finally revealed to be the narrator of *Beatus ille*.

16 See Chapter 2, p. 53.

17 Darman is no doubt recalling Alfred Hitchcock's 1940 film *Rebecca*, directed by David O. Selznick and based on the novel *Rebecca* by Daphne du Maurier.

18 "As the novelist actualizes the world of his imagination through words, so the reader—from those same words—manufactures in reverse a literary universe that is as much his creation as it is the novelist's" (Hutcheon, *Narcissistic* 27).

19 Jonathan Culler provides a critique similar to Freud's. He claims that Iser's "dualism cannot be sustained: the distinction between text and reader, fact and interpretation, or determined and undetermined breaks down" (*On Deconstruction* 75). However, he adds that "[w]e employ such distinctions all the time because our stories require them" (77).

20 See pp. 135–154 of Genette's *Narrative Discourse Revisited*, entitled "Implied Author, Implied Reader?"

21 Iser distinguishes between his theory of reader *response* and theories of reader *reception*: the former "has its roots in the text" while the latter "always deals with existing readers, whose reactions testify to certain historically conditioned experiences of literature" (*Act* x).

22 Jonathan Culler believes that "notions of an ideal reader or a superreader ought to be avoided. To speak of an ideal reader is to forget that reading has a history" (*Pursuit* 51).

CHAPTER FOUR

Intertextualizing the Popular

> No hay palabra que no sea una cita.
> (*El Robinson urbano*)

In the previous chapter, we have seen that Muñoz Molina's texts are essentially reader-oriented in that they engage the active participation of the extratextual reader—through concrete strategies such as gaps of indeterminacy and delaying maneuvers which heighten both mystery and suspense—and also use characters to represent inscribed readers who construct their own versions of reality through "reading" the world as if it were a text:

> hay que escribir las novelas exactamente igual que se leen, como si uno fuera el lector. Yo, cuando escribo, pienso siempre en la manera de conducir al lector proponiéndole túneles con una luz al fondo que a veces apago. Y es que yo, ante todo, me considero lector. (Gutiérrez n. pag.)

Muñoz Molina's writings also reflect his assimilation of a vast artistic tradition, and his allusions include authors from Spain (Cervantes, Salinas, Cernuda), Latin America (Bioy Casares, Borges, Onetti), France (Verne, Flaubert, Baudelaire), England (Chesterton, Conan Doyle, Graham Greene), and the United States (Poe, Scott Fitzgerald, Faulkner).[1] Consequently, any analysis of his work must take into consideration the concept of intertextuality and its relation to reading.

Intertextuality

According to Heinrich Plett, intertextuality "is a fashionable term, but almost everybody who uses it understands it somewhat differently" (3). In its most general sense, intertextuality refers to the fact that every text—in Foucault's words—"is caught up in a system of references to other books, other texts, other sentences: it is a node within a network" (*Archaeology* 23). Intertextuality proposes that texts are not the products of a monological discourse but rather "tissues" or "mosaics"[2] of quotations from other sources, whether these be verbal, visual or acoustic.[3] Readers of Muñoz Molina will find no difficulty in immediately spotting such quotations, as many of the author's titles are taken directly from well-known poems, novels, paintings and films: *Beatus ille* (Horace), *Beltenebros* (Rodríguez de Montalvo), *El jinete polaco* (Rembrandt), "Donde habite el olvido" (Cernuda), "Razón de amor" (Salinas), "Manhattan Transfer" (Dos Passos), "El ángel exterminador" (Buñuel), "Todos los fuegos el fuego" (Cortázar), "La estación florida" (Góngora), etc.

Muñoz Molina often uses intertextual quotations for a specifically parodic effect, as in the first article of *Diario del Nautilus*, which recounts the true story of a French woman, Simone, involved in a legal battle in order to gain the right to be fertilized with the preserved semen of her deceased lover. The article's title—"La memoria en donde ardía"—is taken from verse 6 of Quevedo's sonnet "Amor constante más allá de la muerte," a poem which like the article describes a love that transcends death. But unlike Quevedo, Muñoz Molina ends on an unexpectedly humorous note:

> Pero si no cede en su empeño y alguna vez alcanza la satisfacción de su deseo, convirtiéndose en súcuba feliz de una reliquia rediviva, las congeladas cenizas que aniden en el vientre de Simone habrán hecho cumplirse el veredicto de Quevedo. Polvo serán, mas polvo enamorado. (*Diario del Nautilus* 15)

Here, a literal quotation—the last sentence is also the last verse of Quevedo's sonnet—is comically resemanticized by using it to refer to the popular colloquial expression for ejaculation: "echar un polvo."

"Septiembre escueto y rosa" (*El Robinson urbano*) offers a similar case of parodic intertextuality which conflates the popular with the erudite. The article eulogizes several members of Granada's younger artistic generation, including the painter Juan Vida and the poets Rafael Juárez and Antonio Carvajal, whose work Muñoz Molina sees as representative of another "[E]dad de plata." To describe these works, an advertising slogan for selling clothes is cited: "el tiempo se hizo escueto y rosa…El invierno 82 huye de las formas obvias, de los colores obvios, de todo lo que es fácil" (*El Robinson urbano* 57). The article ends by juxtaposing the advertisement's message with a phrase from José Lezama Lima's essay "Mitos y cansancio clásico:"

> La frágil edad de plata que tal vez se avecina huirá, como la moda de otoño invierno, de las formas obvias, de los colores obvios, de todo lo que es fácil, porque—lo hemos aprendido de Lezama Lima—sólo lo difícil es estimulante. (59)

In both articles, unmodified quotations from Quevedo and Lezama Lima are displaced from their original context, a process that ironically subverts the traditional separation of erudite and popular texts. These and other examples demonstrate that Muñoz Molina's eclectic readings do not exclude popular forms that until recently have been considered as marginal to the Western artistic tradition. He made this clear in an interview in which he situated the American hard-boiled novelist Raymond Chandler and the Spanish popular singer Concha Piquer alongside Miguel de Cervantes and James Joyce:

> me siento como el heredero de una fortuna inmensa porque reclamo toda la tradición para mí, toda la tradición y toda la vanguardia. Reclamo desde Cervantes hasta Joyce, desde Chandler a las canciones de Concha Piquer. (Martín Gil 26)

Although there is lack of agreement among theorists of intertextuality over the role of the reader, it would seem that the effectiveness of intertextuality ultimately depends on the extratextual reader's knowledge and processing of the author's intertexts. As Linda Hutcheon affirms, "the locus of textual appropriation is the reader, and not the author" ("Literary" 231), for "[i]ntertextuality is a function of reading, of 'decoding.'" (233). This supposes, however, that the reader is aware of the intertext:

> The receiver, i.e. the listener or reader, who comes across a quotation text, may either notice the quotations or he may not. If he overlooks them, the text misses its purpose which consists in opening up dialogues between pre-texts and quotation texts. (Plett 15)

In the two articles by Muñoz Molina cited above, the author ensures that his readers will recognize the quoted intertexts. In the first, Quevedo's poem is one that most Spaniards who have completed high-school have had to read and often to memorize.[4] In the second, since most readers are not familiar with Lezama Lima's essays, the author makes a point of identifying his source: "lo hemos aprendido de Lezama Lima." Similarly, although most Spanish readers will have some acquaintance with the poetry of García Lorca, in "Luna de los escaparates" the author clearly identifies the Lorca poem from which he uses a phrase to describe the mannequins in a shop window: "Como Antoñito el Camborio, las maniquíes de las tiendas se mueren siempre de perfil" (*Diario del Nautilus* 28). Muñoz Molina has commented on this deliberate identification of his intertexts: "para que yo haga una cita, la hago explícita" (Rich 1992).

Intertextuality is not only a matter of appropriating material signs—the case of direct quotations—but also of borrowing conventions and structural rules, which Plett refers to as "generic intertextuality" (24). Hans Robert Jauss does not use the term intertextuality, but makes a similar point by citing the canonical example of *Don Quijote*:

> The new text evokes for the reader (listener) the horizons of expectations and rules familiar from earlier texts, which are then varied, corrected, changed or just reproduced.... Thus Cervantes in *Don Quijote* fosters the expectations of the old tales of knighthood, which the adventures of his last knight then parody seriously. (17)

Like Cervantes's *Don Quijote*—which not coincidentally is quoted from in both *Beatus ille* and *Beltenebros*—Muñoz Molina's texts often exploit the reader's expectations of both popular and erudite genres by self-consciously intertextualizing them.

Melodrama, detective fiction, and film

Muñoz Molina's fascination with popular narratives began at an early age. One of his most vivid memories is that of listening to and reading *folletines*.[5] In "El reino de las voces" he recalls how as a young boy he would listen to the *folletines* of Guillermo Sautier Casaseca on the radio, a scene which he would later incorporate in *El jinete polaco*.[6] Muñoz Molina is also an avid fan of detective novels and crime thrillers, and in "Lectura y adicción" compares the effects of reading them to that of taking drugs:

> Con cada nueva novela que leía los efectos eran más rápidos y más indudables, como los de ciertas drogas y, ahora, cuando termino una, al buscar la siguiente noto ya la impaciencia del adicto.

In the same article, he analyzes this literary "addiction" and comes to the following conclusion:

> No leemos novelas policiales para descubrir cosas que ignorábamos ni por amor a la sorpresa, sino exactamente por la razón contraria: para descubrir lo que sabemos de sobra, para poseer la gélida certidumbre de que no nos llevaremos ni una sola sorpresa... Leemos novelas policiales por la misma razón que nos hace frecuentar a unos pocos amigos; porque no hay nada en ellos que no sea delicadamente previsible...

Muñoz Molina's explanation is analogous to John Cawelti's thesis that the reader's need for the familiar is a distinctive characteristic of formula stories (like the detective novel), which "have highly predictable structures that guarantee the fulfillment of conventional expectations" (1). According to Cawelti, "[a]udiences find satisfaction and a basic emotional security in a familiar form" (9).

Along with *folletines* and detective novels, Muñoz Molina has a great appreciation for cinema, and like many of his generation saw scores of Hollywood films which inundated Spain during the post-war period.[7] Although it was not until the late 1970s that translations of the "hard-boiled" detective novels of Dashiell Hammet and Raymond Chandler were made available to the Spanish public, their offshoot, *film noir*, had become immensely popular during the first decades of the post-war period.[8] Testifying to his love for the cinema, Muñoz Molina wrote that "Casi nada que me importe está fuera de las novelas y los cines" ("Noticia de una tentativa").

Intertextuality and film in "El invierno en Lisboa"

Muñoz Molina exploits mystery and suspense to engage his readers, and the hermeneutic code of the detective story is central to *Beatus ille*, in which Minaya solves the mystery of Mariana's murder and discovers the narrator's identity. However, the temporal fragmentation of the narrative and its multiple points of view makes *Beatus ille* a difficult text to read, and although it was awarded the *Premio Icaro*, its initial readership was fairly limited. Muñoz Molina's second novel, *El invierno en Lisboa*, differs radically from the first. Whereas the narrative style of *Beatus ille* is more indebted to William Faulkner and Henry James, *El invierno en Lisboa* is a homage to Raymond Chandler and Alfred Hitchcock. The novel is in fact Muñoz Molina's first full-length exercise in intertextualizing the popular.

Commenting on *El invierno en Lisboa*, the author said "no se trata en absoluto de una novela negra" (Salabert n. pag.). Nevertheless, the novel shares certain characteristics of the popular hard-boiled detective novel of the 1940s: its plot unfolds in urban settings (San Sebastián, Madrid, Paris, Berlin, Lisbon), and the pursuit of a stolen painting by Bruce Malcolm, Toussaints Morton and Lucrecia recalls a similar quest by Gutman, Cairo, and Brigid O'Shaugnessy in Dashiell Hammet's *The Maltese Falcon*. Like Sam Spade's or the Continental Op's, Biralbo's life is constantly in danger, and there are two dramatic scenes in which he narrowly escapes death at the hands of Malcolm and Morton. *El invierno en Lisboa* also uses visual motifs that conjure up the world of *film noir*, including Biralbo's run-down hotel, the neon light outside his window, and the cold and rainy streets of Madrid. However, Lucrecia is not a scheming *femme fatale*, and unlike the hard-boiled private eye, Biralbo is not involved in a personal crusade for justice.[9] The *novela negra* and *film noir* are intertexts of a work in which danger and suspense are merely the backdrop for what is primarily a love story cast in the form of a *bildungsroman*.

Film is first introduced as an intertext when the narrator visits Biralbo at the latter's hotel and says "La recepción de su hotel era como el vestíbulo de uno de esos cines antiguos" (16). (The same description is later used for Billy Swann's hospital, in which "colgaban globos de luz sucios de polvo, como en los cines antiguos" [114]). On returning home, the narrator begins listening to a recording by Swann and Biralbo, which evokes for him images of a movie he has seen:

> Constantemente la música me acuciaba hacia la revelación de un recuerdo, calles abandonadas en la noche, un resplandor de focos al otro lado de las esquinas, sobre fachadas con columnas y terraplenes de derribos, hombres que huían y que se perseguían alargados por sus sombras, con revólveres y sombreros calados y grandes abrigos como el de Biralbo.
>
> Pero ese recuerdo que agravaron la soledad y la música no pertenece a mi vida, estoy seguro, sino a una película que tal vez vi en mi infancia y cuyo título nunca llegaré a saber. (21–22)

The narrator's imaginative vision reflects Muñoz Molina's belief that cinema has profoundly affected the modern psyche: "nuestra imaginación [está] contaminada por el cine" ("La cara del pasado"), given that we interpret the world through a filter of our previous "readings," which include the films we have seen. The narrator's memory and imagination are indeed "contaminated by the cinema," for he admits that his "recuerdo...pertenece...a una película" (21) and the images that he evokes are typical motifs of *film noir*: abandoned streets, a stark contrast between light ("focos") and dark ("sombras") and men with revolvers dressed in hats and overcoats.[10]

Throughout *El invierno en Lisboa*, the narrator's imaginary visions of events are described as if they were scenes from a Hollywood film. When Biralbo tells him how Bruce Malcolm had been spying on him and Lucrecia, the narrator comments:

> de pronto yo había visto, desde arriba, como se ve en las películas, una calle vulgar de San Sebastián en la que un hombre, parado en la acera, levantaba los ojos hacia una ventana, con las manos en los bolsillos, con una pistola... (33)

The narrator even interprets a photograph of Billy Swann in cinematic terms:

> Se veía en ella a un hombre alto y envejecido, con la cara angulosa medio tapada por el ala de uno de esos sombreros que usaban los actores secundarios en las películas antiguas. (46)

The narrator is not the only character who uses film as an intertextual frame of reference. When Floro Bloom discovers two glasses and three lipstick-stained cigarette butts in an ashtray, he immediately deduces that Biralbo and Lucrecia have visited his bar when it was closed, and ironically calls the two "Fantasmas" (82). He then asks the narrator, "*Phantom Lady*. ¿Has visto esa película?" (82). The reader need not have seen the film to appreciate Floro Bloom's irony, but those who have will recall that one of its most famous scenes is an after-hours jam session, an indirect reference to Biralbo's spontaneous performance for Lucrecia the night before.[11]

Like the narrator and Floro Bloom, Biralbo and Lucrecia also interpret the world through a cinematic filter. When Biralbo takes leave of Lucrecia, who is leaving with Malcolm for Paris, she asks him:

> "Has visto cómo llueve?" Yo [Biralbo] le contesté que así siempre llueve en las películas cuando la gente va a despedirse.... Me preguntó por qué sabía yo que aquel encuentro era el último. "Pues por las películas", le dije, "cuando llueve tanto es que alguien se va a ir para siempre." (38)

Biralbo's commentary is an intertextual reference to a number of Hollywood films, but evokes in particular the scene in *Casablanca* in which Rick (Humphrey Bogart) is left standing helplessly in the rain at a train station with Ilse's (Ingrid Bergman) goodbye note in his hand.[12] *Casablanca* is used as an explicit intertext when Biralbo goes with Lucrecia to the Lady Bird late one night:

> Porque habían nacido para fugitivos amaron siempre las películas, la música, las ciudades extranjeras. Lucrecia se acodó en la barra, probó el whisky y dijo, burlándose de sí misma y de Biralbo y de lo que estaba a punto de decir y amándolo sobre todas las cosas:
> —Tócala otra vez. Tócala otra vez para mí.
> —Sam, dijo él, calculando la risa y la complicidad—. Samtiago Biralbo. (80)

Muñoz Molina has compared the intertextuality of film in *El invierno en Lisboa* to the use of the novel of chivalry in *Don Quijote*:

> "Muy poca gente se ha dado cuenta", afirma, "de que el cine en ese libro viene a ser lo que las novelas de caballería al Quijote: forma parte de la trama, del carácter de los personajes, que viven como si fuesen los protagonistas de una película…" (Arias)

The author's observation is true, but should be qualified. Unlike Don Quijote, who believes unequivocally that he is a knight-errant, at the moment when Biralbo and Lucrecia are in the bar they self-consciously play the roles of *Casablanca*'s Sam and Ilse, "calculando la risa y la complicidad." Muñoz Molina admitted as much when he said: "Biralbo, el protagonista, está haciendo una defensa de la ironía como antídoto contra el absolutismo de los sentimientos" (Ribas 52). This is the irony to which Umberto Eco refers when he describes the postmodern man who is incapable of saying "I love you madly" to a woman,

> because he knows that she knows (and that she knows that he knows) that these words have already been written by Barbara Cartland. Still, there is a solution. He can say, "As Barbara Cartland would put it, I love you madly." ("Postmodernism" 67)

Biralbo and Lucrecia mirror Eco's postmodern lovers, for both are aware that they are mimicking a cinematic discourse, and that Lucrecia is in fact saying, "As Ilse would put it, play it again, Sam."

In its use of film as an explicit intertext, *El invierno en LIsboa* is a metafictional text that self-consciously foregrounds the use of one genre for the creation of another. Nothing is known of Biralbo's past, and the narrator underscores this by saying that the musician "aspiraba a ser como esos héroes de las películas cuya biografía comienza al mismo tiempo que la acción y no tienen pasado" (40). Toussaints Morton "[h]ablaba exactamente igual que los negros de las películas" (52), and Maraña carries a revolver "más largo que Biralbo había visto nunca, incluso en las películas" (176). When Biralbo manages to escape from Bruce Malcolm and Toussaints Morton, he sees himself as an actor in a film—"Biralbo salió de espaldas, acordándose de que era así como salían los héroes de las películas" (141). The novel ends as the narrator watches Lucrecia disappear in the rain, "como si nunca hubiera existido" (187), a final comment on the cinematic fictionality not only of Lucrecia but also of the other characters.

I would like to return for a moment to the author's statement cited previously that *El invierno en Lisboa* "no se trata en absoluto de una novela negra." There is some truth to this, for although most of the cinematic intertexts such as *Phantom Lady* are evidently taken from the world of *film noir*, *Casablanca* is a romantic melodrama. At the same time, popular intertexts are blended with erudite ones, beginning with the opening epigraph from Flaubert's novel *L'Éducation sentimentale*. Therefore, the novel should also be read as a love story and *bildungsroman*, in which the epigraph suggests an association between Biralbo and Lucrecia's love affair and the doomed relationship between Frédéric Moreau and Marie Arnoux.[13] There are other literary allusions such as the name "Floro Bloom" which recalls James Joyce's *Ulysses* and Bloom's pseudonym "Henry *Flower*." The bartender in *El invierno en Lisboa* examines an ashtray "como si sostuviera una patena" (82) and raises a whisky bottle "solemnemente entre las dos manos" (85) while speaking in Latin. This recalls the opening scene of *Ulysses* in which Buck Mulligan holds his shaving bowl up and intones "Introibo ad altare Dei" (Joyce 3). Nevertheless, film remains the predominant intertext of *El invierno en Lisboa*, providing both the melodrama of *Casablanca* and the suspense of Alfred Hitchcock's movies. As the author himself admitted, "he integrado elementos cinematográficos, con una gran influencia, por ejemplo, de Hitchcock" (Salabert).

Intertextuality and conventions of reading
Intertextuality includes both direct quotations and the appropriation of conventions and rules: "intertextual structures...may be of the order of the message or of the order of the code. Texts are made out of...the conventions of genre" (Frow 45). I will now discuss briefly how Muñoz Molina plays with his readers' generic expectations by intertextualizing the formal detective novel and the hard-boiled thriller.

In Chapter 3 I noted that *Beatus ille* intertextualizes the formal detective story by portraying Minaya as an amateur detective and expanding on the genre by presenting not one but two mysteries: the identity of Mariana's murderer and that of the anonymous narrator. *Beatus ille* is therefore faithful to the genre of the detective novel insofar as it fulfills reader expectations by providing solutions to two enigmas. However, it also subverts reader expectations in one important way. Besides its obvious debt to the detective novel, *Beatus ille* is a work of historiographic metafiction that challenges the authority of "official" history through its foregrounding of the impossibility of reconstructing the past: the "crónica impasible" for which Minaya is searching is shown to be a chimera, the product of a subjective and ontologically ambivalent narrator. Solana underscores this when he tells Minaya, "acaso la historia que usted ha encontrado sólo es una entre varias posibles" (277). In doing so, Solana denies one of the very foundations of the formal detective novel—narrative closure—and unlike a detective story, the "case" is not in fact "closed." Reader expectations in *Beatus ille* are fulfilled through the detective novel's traditional use of mysteries and clues, but at the same time subverted by a self-consciously conditional ending. The conclusion of *El invierno en Lisboa* also subverts conventional expectations of a final resolution. As in *The Maltese Falcon*, the plot revolves around a priceless object over which the characters are prepared to lie, cheat, and murder, but unlike the falcon, the object is never seen (Lucrecia sells the Cézanne painting) and the novel ends *in media res*, with Lucrecia searching for Biralbo to warn him of the danger he is in, and with Malcolm and Morton still in pursuit of Lucrecia, Biralbo and the painting.

The first sentence of *Beltenebros* activates traditional reading codes of the hard-boiled thriller and spy novel: "Vine a Madrid para matar a un hombre a quien no había visto nunca" (7). The reader is prepared for a conventional thriller, and the novel does in effect fulfil traditional expectations of the genre in that it portrays a professional assassin who moves in a decaying urban setting, a panorama of shady characters (some with pseudonyms), a *femme fatale* who drugs the protagonist, and two spectacular chase scenes. Nevertheless, like the two novels which preceded it, *Beltenebros* does not confine its focus to the mimetic world of the story but self-consciously underscores its own fictionality, in stark contrast to the realistic pretensions of the hard-boiled detective novel. Whereas the latter demands the reader's unconditional acceptance of the diegetic world portrayed, *Beltenebros* continually qualifies this reality. In airports "ni el tiempo ni el espacio son del todo reales" (13), a cathedral seen from a hotel window is "tan irreal y cercana como un espejismo" (28), the events of Darman's past "tenían una irrealidad de pasado lejano" (143), and the streets of Madrid are "las calles de un Madrid irreal" (156).

The explicit references to fictionality in *Beltenebros* recall Jorge Luis Borges's dictum in "El milagro secreto" that "la irrealidad...es condición del arte" (Borges 152), and there are unmistakable Borgesian intertexts throughout the novel.[14] Destiny is treated as inexorable ("una invisible corriente más poderosa que mi voluntad" [*Beltenebros* 57]), time as circular ("viaje circular" [130, 186]), and ever-present are two typical motifs of Borges, doubles and mirrors, both of which indicate a characteristically Borgesian rejection of the unified Cartesian subject ("Yo mismo me multiplicaba invisiblemente en otros hombres" [41]). Through intertextual allusions to Borges[15] and the status of his characters as fictions, Muñoz Molina creates a double-coded text which can be read both as a conventional hard-boiled thriller and as a self-conscious metafiction in which Rebeca Osorio's novels are a *mise en abîme* of the text itself.

Unlike the formal detective novel, in which emphasis is placed on the solution to a mystery, the hard-boiled detective novel is more concerned with the role of the detective, which John Cawelti calls "the subordination of the drama of solution to the detective's quest for the discovery and accomplishment of justice" (142). This "shift in the underlying archetype...from the pattern of mystery to that of heroic adventure" (142) implies a change in narrative strategies. Whereas the formal detective novel is either narrated in third person or by a character other than the detective —Holmes's Watson—the hard-boiled novels of Raymond Chandler are narrated by the detective himself, and Muñoz Molina follows Chandler by using a first-person narrator in *Beltenebros*.

Costumbrismo and the *folletín* in *Los misterios de Madrid*

Los misterios de Madrid is Muñoz Molina's intertextual *mélange* of two nineteenth-century genres, the *folletín* and the *cuadro de costumbres*. Its title recalls not only the best-selling *feuilleton Les Mystères de Paris* (1842) by Eugène Sue, but also the Spanish imitation entitled *Misterios de Madrid*, published in 1846 by Ayguals de Izco and his brother.[16] The narrative technique and themes of Muñoz Molina's version are characteristic of the *folletín*: the use of cutting to engage the reader, a mysterious crime, and a melodramatic plot which includes the common *folletín* motif of a woman who claims her fortune as the illegitimate daughter of an aristocrat. Because the novel portrays both the geography and inhabitants of Madrid, however, it can also be read as a contemporary version of the *cuadro de costumbres*.

From the moment that Quesada arrives in Madrid, the narrator presents a series of characters representative of the urban population. Like a *costumbrista* author, the narrator describes them as character-types rather than as individuals. His vivid and picturesque portraits include those of a *macarra*,[17] a taxi-driver, and a group of gypsies:

> [Lorencito Quesada chocó] con un joven de melena muy larga que casi medía dos metros y llevaba una camiseta negra con una calavera dibujada en el pecho. (29)

> [E]l conductor, mascando uno de esos cigarillos falsos con que se alivian los ex fumadarores, murmuraba en voz baja venenosos juramentos contra las autoridades o prorrumpía en carcajadas al oír los chistes que alguien contaba en la radio con acento gallego. (40)

> En las puertas de las chabolas permanecían sentadas, con la costura o el rosario en el regazo, gitanas viejas con refajos de luto y pañolones negros a la cabeza, algunos de ellos ceñidos por los auriculares de un *walkman*... (121)

The goal of *costumbrista* authors was to to document a series of social changes that Spain was undergoing in the nineteenth century as a result of increasing urbanization (Zavala 338). Faced with the radical changes brought by modernization, the *cuadro de costumbres* presented a nostalgic vision of a way of life that was seen as slowly disappearing. José Montesinos writes that *costumbrista* authors intended to

> dar fe de un cambio, de una revolución, de una evolución que ha transformado la faz de todo el país...y desahogar, entregándose al recuerdo, la nostalgia de todo lo desaparecido y olvidado. (*Costumbrismo* 44)

In the case of Mesonero Romanos, a leading *costumbrista* author, nostalgia was a symptom of social conservatism:

> Como Larra, los costumbristas eran penosamente conscientes de que la sociedad española estaba en una fase de rápida transición... Pero, al contrario de Larra...tenían una visión ampliamente conservadora, al menos en la literatura.... Era inevitable que, al describir el modo de vivir típicamente español, los costumbristas defendieran los valores tradicionales. (Shaw 84)

Muñoz Molina parodies the conservative ethos of the *costumbrista* authors by portraying both the narrator and Quesada as arch-traditionalists who are repelled by the changes that urbanization have brought to Madrid. Quesada is a member of "nuestra Acción Católica" (28), and is aghast at the thought of Spain's racial purity being threatened by a flood of foreign immigrants:

> ¿Cómo no iba a estar lleno de peligros una ciudad poblada de moros, negros y chinos? Al menos el taxista pertenecía a la minoritaria raza blanca. Como suele predicar en Mágina el párroco de la Trinidad, que está enfrente de El Sistema Métrico, el hombre blanco se extingue por culpa de la píldora, de la sodomía y del aborto. (39)
>
> [S]ólo veía a su alrededor mendigos, tullidos, negros, marroquíes, indios de América del Sur que tocaban bombos y flautas, gente patibularia que trapicheaba en las esquinas, asesinos y salteadores en potencia. (58)

What distinguishes Muñoz Molina's parody of the *cuadro de costumbres* is that the traditionalism of both the narrator and Quesada is the target of irony, and their conservative ideals are constantly exposed to ridicule. At one point, Quesada is asked the time by a well-dressed gentleman "con una pequeña insignia patriótica o religiosa en el ojal" (60–61). However, despite the man's appearance,

> aquel señor tan educado, que le había inspirado tanta confianza, le estaba proponiendo lo que él mismo, valientemente, sin tapujos, llamó después un acto sexual contra natura… (61)

Insofar as it ironically pokes fun at both traditional Catholicism and the political ideals of the Franco regime, *Los misterios de Madrid* has less in common with Mesonero Romano's benevolent vision of *castizo* Spain than with José Mariano de Larra's virulent social criticism. In fact, when Quesada is accosted by his friend Pepín Godino, the scene recalls an analagous one in Larra's "El castellano viejo," in which the narrator is also unpleasantly surprised from behind by his friend Braulio. Lara's Braulio, who flaunts his patriotism and religiosity—"tiene una cintita atada al ojal y una crucecita a la sombra de la solapa…. Es tal su patriotismo que dará todas las lindezas del extranjero por un dedo de su país" (Larra 314)—is strikingly similar to Pepín, who "[e]n la solapa de su chaqueta llevaba siempre un escudo de nuestra ciudad" (*Los misterios de Madrid* 51). The "respectable" gentleman who attempts to seduce Quesada also wears "una pequeña insignia patriótica o religiosa en el ojal." It is therefore highly probable that Muñoz Molina had Larra in mind when creating the figures of Pepín and the gentleman who propositions Quesada.

To underscore his intertextualization of nineteenth-century forms, the narrator of *Los misterios de Madrid* uses a rhetorical and often pedantic style typical of the epoch, adding cliched expressions taken from contemporary advertisements and pulp fiction:

> [Qesada tomaba] una copa de quina San Clemente, bebida ésta que *por sus cualidades nutritivas ha gozado siempre de su preferencia*. (9)
>
> [Quesada] se encontró en lo que había sido el comedor de la pensión en *los tiempos dorados* del señor Rojo. (38)
>
> Lorencito miró las pistolas de Bocarrape y del Bimbollo, temiendo que si se movía *escupieran plomo* contra él. (109; emphases added)

Commenting on his self-conscious use of an anachronistic style, Muñoz Molina remarked in an interview (Rich 1994) that he had attempted the same discursive register in *El jinete polaco* to recount the life of don Mercurio, a doctor who arrives in Mágina during Amadeo de Saboya's reign:

> [Don Mercurio] tenía un sentido casi hiriente del ridículo ajeno, y no podía menos que presenciar con desagrado la brutalidad de los excesos alcohólicos, lacra funesta de las clases humildes y obstáculo para su redención. (*El jinete polaco* 37)

Don Mercurio's moralistic pronouncements, typical of a *costumbrista* narrator, echo those of Lorencito Quesada, who like the doctor refers to alcoholism as "una lacra social" (*Los misterios de Madrid* 30).

In addition to parodying *costumbrismo*, *Los misterios de Madrid* also humorously intertextualizes a commonplace of nineteenth-century romanticism. When Quesada bumps his groin on a prie-dieu in a darkened church,

> antes que gritar o que llevarse las manos a la parte herida, que era de las más blandas de su anatomía, prefirió apretar los dientes y *dejar que una lágrima se le deslizara por la mejilla temblona*. (13; emphasis added)

Russel Sebold has noted the tendency of romantic heroes to cry with only a single tear, and the description of Quesada parallels that of Espronceda's Leonor in *Sancho Saldaña*: "una lágrima se desprendió a pesar suyo por sus mejillas" (qtd. in Sebold 187).

Whereas the characters in *El invierno de Lisboa* interpret reality in cinematic terms, Quesada sees himself as the participant in both a detective and an adventure novel. He carefully saves an envelope for this reason:

> consideró que era vital no destruir ninguna prueba, ni las que parecieran menos importantes, pues con frecuencia son éstas las que sirven para averiguar la clave de un enigma... (34)

When the shop assistant tells Quesada that one of the villains was carrying a strange knife, Quesada identifies it as a "cris malayo" although "no había visto nunca dicha arma, pero tenía noticias exactas sobre ella gracias a las novelas de Emilio Salgari" (69).

Despite the complex and melodramatic plot of *Los misterios de Madrid* characteristic of the nineteenth-century *folletín*, a conventional ending is unexpectedly subverted. In a typical *folletín*, love triumphs and the villain—invariably an evil aristocrat—is punished. In contrast, at the end of *Los misterios de Madrid*, Olga rejects Quesada and don Sebastián Guadalimar escapes punishment. John Cawelti notes that melodramatic forms like the *folletín* assert "the essential 'rightness' of the world order" (45). Quesada does in fact restore order by recovering the processional figure, but in doing so ensures the continuing power of the aristocracy in Mágina, an ironic commentary on the "rightness" of this order: don Sebastián has been exposed as a criminal, but continues—along with his wife and her daughter—to preside over the Holy Week procession.

Los misterios de Madrid is a metafictional text in which Quesada, a journalist, refers to how he will eventually publish the story. At the beginning of the novel he waits to be received by don Sebastián:

> imaginando de antemano el modo en que la contaría en un reportaje a doble página de *Singladura*, o quién sabe si en unas *Memorias* que sólo en su vejez se decidiría a escribir… (11)

In addition to self-consciously mirroring the publication of *Los misterios de Madrid* in *El País*, this passage also points to Quesada as the author of his own story, for the narrator is merely Quesada's transcriber. The novel ends as Quesada begins to tell his story to the narrator, and the last sentence of the novel is also the first: "Daban las once en el reloj de la plaza del General Orduña" (188). As a metafictional text, this novel inscribes its own narrative process.

Metafiction and intertextuality complement each other in Muñoz Molina's works, for his characters are self-consciously portrayed as inscribed authors and readers as they interpret reality through a filter of intertexts. Because reality is always (inter)textually mediated, it becomes an elusive concept, and in an article on the painter Juan Vida, Muñoz Molina writes:

> el mundo real—que para él es un mundo imaginario, *pues sólo lo conoce por las páginas de los periódicos*, por el brillo satinado de las revistas de arte—es tan inalcanzable para él como para un náufrago varado en una isla desierta. ("La mirada que pinta;" emphasis added)

As we have already seen, in attempting to apprehend reality, Muñoz Molina's characters are constantly frustrated by the mediation of memory and the Quixotic contamination of their imaginations by fiction. *El jinete polaco* and *El dueño del secreto* continue to demonstrate the mediating effects of memory and imagination, but in a form which the author had not attempted previously—that of the fictive autobiography.

Notes

[1] I have mentioned only a few of the well-known authors that Muñoz Molina has cited in his work. A complete list would include many more.

[2] Roland Barthes refers to a text as "a tissue of quotations" ("Death" 146), and Julia Kristeva writes that any text "is constructed as a mosaic of quotations" ("Word" 37).

[3] See Plett (20).

[4] A personal incident first made me aware of this. In 1986 one of my Spanish friends (who was not a student of literature) wrote the entire Quevedo sonnet cited above from memory on a paper napkin.

[5] The *folletín*—a Spanish version of the French *feuillleton*—was immensely popular throughout the nineteenth century and has survived until the present in the form of the *novela rosa*.

[6] In *El jinete polaco* the protagonist, Manuel, listens to the *folletines* of Xavier de Montepin (20), and later refers to "aquellos folletines que mi abuelo nos leía en las noches de invierno" (89). In *Beatus ille*, Manuel describes Solana as a young boy: "En su casa había un solo libro. Se llamaba, me acuerdo, *Rosa María o la Flor de los amores*, un folletín en tres volúmenes que Solana leyó a los diez años y por el que guardó siempre una especie de gratitud" (49).

[7] "Los *cinéfilos* (palabra que tendría rápida consagración) de los años sesenta y setenta...confiesan sin rebozo haber devorado largas sesiones dobles de cine norteamericano" (Tuñón de Lara 358).

[8] "Las versiones cinematográficas de las novelas más importantes de Hammet y Chandler alcanzaron gran éxito en las primeras décadas de la postguerra española.... No es hasta los finales de la década de los setenta que las novelas mismas se dan a conocer al público en versiones españolas, tarea que lleva a cabo en especial la editorial Bruguera, ayudada por Alianza en cuanto a las obras de Dashiell Hammett y Barral para las de Raymond Chandler" (Amell, "La novela negra" 92–93). In "Los detectives," Muñoz Molina notes that "Hacia la mitad de los años setenta los detectives privados se vinieron a vivir a Espana."

[9] "[The hard-boiled detective novel's] central problem is a version of the quest, both a search for truth and an attempt to eradicate evil" (Grella, "Hard-Boiled" 104).

10 For some of these motifs, see the chapter on "Black Film" in Higham and Greenberg's *Hollywood in the Forties*, pp. 19–36 and Place and Peterson's article "Some Visual Motifs of Film Noir."

11 *Phantom Lady* (1944), based on a novel by William Irish, was directed by Robert Siodmack.

12 *Casablanca* (1942) was directed by Michael Curtiz and written by Julius J. Epstein, Philip G. Epstein, and Howard Koch.

13 Muñoz Molina has said "La novela trata de un aprendizaje" (Ribas 52). Although it may be coincidental, in Flaubert's novel Marie Arnoux's husband sells paintings and art magazines, while Bruce Malcolm traffics in stolen paintings.

14 The author has admitted that "a Borges le debo todo, absolutamente todo" (Vidal-Folch n. pag.).

15 Bernal's description of Andrade as "El traidor [que] huye convertido en héroe" (49) probably refers to Borges's short story "Tema del traidor y del héroe" in *Ficciones*.

16 For an overview of detective stories written in Spanish, see Ian Michael's "From Scarlet Study to Novela Negra."

17 Víctor León in his *Diccionario de Argot Español* (3rd ed. Madrid: Alianza, 1983) gives several definitions of "macarra" including "chulo de barrio," "individuo follonista y sin escrúpulos" and "punk."

CHAPTER FIVE

Self-Conscious Realism and the (Auto)biographical Mode

> En los libros siempre se cuenta uno a sí mismo. (Muñoz Molina)

Muñoz Molina's fourth novel, *El jinete polaco*, is a fictional autobiography/biography in which the protagonist, Manuel, is a thinly disguised "portrait of the artist."[1] At the same time, the novel is a memoir which functions as a highly verisimilar chronicle of an epoch. The author has commented on this historical aspect of the novel:

> Mi novela es histórica porque trata de un devenir histórico, del devenir de lo que ha ocurrido en España, del tránsito de una realidad rural precapitalista a una sociedad de consumo. (García, Angeles 26)

The events occur over a period that spans more than a century—from the 1870s to the narrator's present in 1991—and *Beatus ille*'s fictional town, Mágina, is once again the primary setting. The novel is composed of three major sections. The first, "El reino de las voces," intersperses scenes of Manuel's family life and infancy in Mágina with the *feuilleton*-inspired story of a doctor, don Mercurio, and the discovery of a mummy in an abandoned house in Mágina. The second, "El jinete en la tormenta," is an account of Manuel's adolescence in Mágina which alternates with the life of Commander Galaz, a veteran of Spain's Civil War and the father of Nadia, the woman with whom Manuel falls in love. The last, "El jinete polaco," relates Manuel's search for Nadia and their reunion in New York, after which Manuel solves the mystery of the mummy and Nadia rejoins him in Mágina.

Like the author's previous novels, *El jinete polaco* continues a focus on memory and imagination as means of reconstructing the past. Manuel and Nadia are aided by photographs and the oral accounts and memories of Mágina's inhabitants, but when Manuel wishes to describe a time "anterior a mi memoria y también a mi vida" (21), he assumes all the powers of a fictional author, inventing freely and admitting at one point that his memory and imagination have become inextricably confused: "imagino cautelosamente el privilegio de inventarme recuerdos que debiera haber poseído.... [L]o que yo supongo invención en realidad es una forma invulnerada de memoria..." (194).

Manuel and Nadia set about the task of reconstructing the story of don Mercurio and the mummy as a traditional historian would—by resorting to eye-witness testimony: "Para no perderse en un laberinto de pasados deciden establecer el principio de todo en el testimonio más antiguo que poseen: el médico joven..." (33). However, the doctor's story is a fourth-hand account, having passed to Ramiro Retratista, then to Commander Galaz, and finally to his daughter Nadia:

> Lo que ocurrió una sola vez...se degrada primero en la memoria del primer testigo y luego en las palabras escuchadas y atesoradas por Ramiro Retratista y transmitidas al comandante Galaz en un futuro en el que ya no vive nadie a cuyo testimonio sea posible recurrir... (32–33)

It is not until the end of the novel that Manuel talks with the doctor's former coachman, Julián, who tells him that Ramiro—an alcoholic photographer described as "muy imaginativo" (98)—had been deceived by don Mercurio's invention of the feuilleton-like story of the mummy:

> a don Mercurio no le costó ningún trabajo engañarlo [a Ramiro] con aquel folletín que le contó para que no siguiera molestándolo: los enmascarados en la noche del martes de carnaval, el coche de caballos, la dama parturienta en la habitación de una criada, el niño que nació muerto, nada de eso era verdad... (564)

Julián then tells Manuel that

> lo único que era verdad es lo que tú supones que era falso, la momia, lo que has visto esta mañana no es lo mismo que encontramos nosotros en el sótano de la Casa de las Torres, sino una copia exacta, y fue don Mercurio quien encargó que la hicieran... (564–5)

Despite Julián's apparent clarification of the story based on his testimony as an eye-witness, its truth is still left in doubt. Manuel describes himself listening to Julián "como cuando escuchaba hablar a mi abuelo Manuel en la mesa camilla" (565), and the grandfather has already been portrayed as a most unreliable narrator, given to fantasy and invention. Cause is therefore given for the reader to suspect that Julián—like Manuel's grandfather—might be inventing the story. More importantly, when the "guardesa" first discovers the mummy, she describes its skin to the Inspector as "tan suave como un melocotón, pero muy pálida, eso sí, *como la cera…*" (66; emphasis added), and when inspector Pérez and others go to investigate, the mummy is described by the narrator as "como una imagen de cera" (68) and by Ramiro Retratista as having a neck "que parecía de cera" (74). A retroactive reading suggests that perhaps the mummy never existed, but was from the beginning the wax figure that Manuel finds in the antique shop. Thus, although one enigma is solved—what happened during Manuel's five hours with Nadia—whether the mummy really existed is left unresolved. The story of the mummy serves to underscore the ambiguous status of any record of the past, as history and fiction become inextricably intertwined.

In addition to its depiction of the negative aspects of Francoism—including grandfather Manuel's internment in a concentration camp, the political activities of the secret police, and social repression ("los siniestros viernes santos franquistas en los que ni siquiera abrían los cines" [526])—*El jinete polaco* also chronicles Spain's rapid economic recovery during the 1960s:

> "¡Casas de veinte pisos!", declamaba mi abuelo Manuel, "¡Cintas magnetofónicas! ¡Máquinas de varear los olivos!" Platos de duralex, muebles de formica…neveras que enfriaban las cosas sin necesidad de cargarlas de hielo, estufas de butano, braseros eléctricos… (248–49)

Social and economic changes occur so rapidly that they seem almost unreal to the townspeople of Mágina. Muñoz Molina has stated that he wanted to avoid the influence of the South American novel when writing this novel, but his descriptions of these changes include explicit intertextual references to Gabriel García Márquez's *Cien años de soledad*.[2] In the latter novel, José Arcadio Buendía tells his wife Ursula "En el mundo están ocurriendo cosas increíbles" (*Cien años* 15), a comment repeated almost literally by cousin Rafael: "En el mundo, muy lejos de Mágina, estaban ocurriendo cosas extraordinarias" (*El jinete* 158). Likewise, José calls ice "el gran invento de nuestro tiempo" (*Cien años* 23), while for grandfather Manuel the gas stove is "el invento del siglo" (*El jinete* 176). Muñoz Molina's novel is historical, but his characters view historical events as bordering on the fantastic.

Muñoz Molina and the autobiographical impulse

Contemporary literary criticism has constantly warned against naive readings which tend to identify the real author with his/her fictional characters, and Muñoz Molina echoed this view when he wrote that "[c]iertos lectores cometen la obscena presunción de vincular la biografía de un escritor a la de sus personajes" ("Byron, the wanderer" XV). However, there is also a danger in adopting a purely intrinsic conception of a text. René Welleck and Austin Warren state that "[t]he whole view that art is self-expression pure and simple, the transcript of personal feelings and experiences, is demonstrably false" (*Theory of Literature* 78), but they add an important qualification:

> The poet's work may be a mask, a dramatized conventionalization, but it is frequently a conventionalization of his own experiences, his own life. If used with a sense of these distinctions, there is use in biographical study. (79)

This concept of the narrative mask is crucial in analyzing Muñoz Molina's fiction, for in addition to the mask ("la máscara") he often uses two other related motifs: one's "other lives" ("otras vidas") and the impostor ("el impostor").

As a youth, Muñoz Molina's creative urge expressed itself in his fantasies of becoming another *persona*: "[uno] imaginaba para sí mismo otra vida y se atribuía otros nombres..." ("Noticia de una tentativa"). Subsequently, he wrote that the essence of literature lies in the author's desire to assume other identities by projecting himself through the lives of his fictional characters: "Una novela es *la otra vida* necesaria que no nos atrevimos a desear" ("Un lugar donde vivir"); "por eso se escriben y se leen novelas, para vivir *otras vidas*" (Cantavella; emphases added). This belief that an author is continually expressing him/herself through a variety of different roles and identities is summed up in a passage from Muñoz Molina's first anthology, *El Robinson urbano*:

> A Robinson lo que le importa no es encontrarse, sino perderse y huir, cambiar de nombre, usar la máscara del Carnaval para irrumpir en las calles dejando al azar de su trazado la elección de las varias vidas posibles que lo están guardando.... Porque el impostor...suele regresar al abrigo de su primera máscara. (34–35)[3]

Given Muñoz Molina's fascination with fictional identities and masks, I believe that there is an implicit autobiographical urge which informs all of his fiction, and that it is not coincidental that his first anthology takes its name from Daniel Defoe's fictional autobiography *Robinson Crusoe*.

There are clear autobiographical references in Muñoz Molina's first novel, *Beatus ille*. Born in Andalusia, from an early age the author learned to detest the drudgery of farm work and the stifling atmosphere of small-town life, both of which he yearned to escape:

> Esa conciencia de haberme escapado del campo, de aquella vida, de la pobreza, me ha dejado el instinto de huir…. Acaso por eso no escribo nada más que de fugitivos.[4]

In *Beatus ille*, Solana's desire to leave Mágina mirrors the author's experience of living in Úbeda:

> Los labios apretados, la rabia oscura y el odio lúcido contra la vida que le negaba esa casa y esa biblioteca, la voluntad de rebelarse contra todo y huir de Mágina y de su padre y de las dos hectáreas de tierra y del porvenir en que su padre quería confinarlo…. [L]o que le hizo apretar los puños…[era]…la conciencia de la sucia escasez en que había nacido y de la fatiga animal del trabajo al que se sabía condenado. (49–50)

Minaya's background is also similar to that of the real author. Like Minaya, on graduating from high-school Muñoz Molina went to Madrid to study journalism at the university. As a student during the final year of Franco's rule, he was once taken prisoner during a political demonstration, a traumatic experience which Minaya also undergoes.[5]

One might well question whether Solana and Minaya are intended to be narrative masks of the real author, given that the need to escape small-town life or being imprisoned for demonstrating against the Franco regime were experiences shared by hundreds (if not thousands) of Spaniards like Solana and Minaya. However, another factor must be taken into account. Muñoz Molina has always taken great care in assigning his characters names—in his article "Lecciones de abismo" he wrote that "el rasgo definitivo de un personaje es su nombre" and in an interview said that "los nombres de los personajes nunca son arbitarios y son, quizá, lo más necesario que tienen los personajes" (Martín Gil 28). I would suggest that the names Jacinto Solana and Minaya are, like the characters they designate, masks which conceal the author's name:[6]

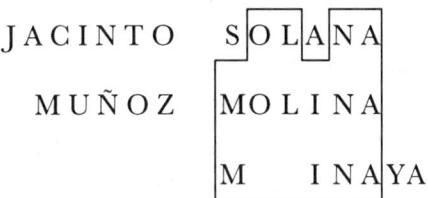

Muñoz Molina's first three novels conceive the past as constantly mediated by the imagination and memory, and consequently imbued with a fictive dimension. But by 1992, the author had begun to grow uncomfortable with his excessive fascination with fiction:

> Como el novelista apócrifo Jacinto Solana, yo me decía que no me importa que una historia sea verdad o mentira, sino que uno sepa contarla. Pero hubo un momento…en que me dí cuenta de que en esa pasión podía encontrarse un veneno y empecé a recelar parcialmente de ella. Había amado y exaltado siempre la imaginación, pero de pronto no estuve seguro de que mi incondicionalidad fuera del todo legítima. (*La realidad de la ficción* 12–13).

> Dar mucha importancia a la literatura, a la música, a las películas…es una enfermedad, y yo creo que he padecido esa enfermedad, ser demasiado literario. (Reyes-Ortiz 26–27)

Muñoz Molina had also become dissatisfied with what he saw as the increasing inverisimilitude of his characters. Commenting on *Beltenebros*, he said of Darman:

> tengo la sensación que esa voz que encontré no era la adecuada, y me duele pensar que por su culpa, o por mi falta de sabiduría, o de paciencia, borró a otras voces que importaban más y que ni el lector ni yo podremos ya oír. Puede que esa voz sea parcialmente falsa porque está contaminada de estilo, porque *no es la voz de un hombre, sino la de una máscara*. (*La realidad de la ficción* 64; emphasis added)

When Manuel in *El jinete polaco* says "he usado mi voz para inventar o mentir o para enmascararme en las voces de los otros" (390), he is referring to his profession as an interpreter. But in light of Muñoz Molina's changing attitude, Manuel's comment may also be seen as a self-critique of the author's previous novels, in which he used a fictional civil war poet (*Beatus ille*), a jazz musician (*El invierno en Lisboa*), and a resistance member (*Beltenebros*) as narrative masks. In *El jinete polaco*, the distance between the author and the narrator's voice is drastically reduced, and the narrator Manuel underscores this when he says

> por primera vez en mi vida soy yo quien cuenta…quien cuenta no para inventar o para esconderse a sí mismo…sino para explicarme todo lo que hasta ahora tal vez nunca entendí, *lo que oculté tras las voces de otros*. Ahora es mi voz la que escucho… (180; emphasis added)

In my opininion, when Muñoz Molina insisted that *El jinete polaco* was more "realistic" than his previous novels, he was referring not only to its verisimilar historical content, but also to the fact that in this novel the narrative mask separating the author from his fictional protagonist, Manuel, approaches almost complete transparency. Since this is also the case in *El dueño del secreto*, I will now discuss the incorporation of autobiographical and biographical strategies in these two works.

Between history and fiction
Insofar as *El jinete polaco* and *El dueño del secreto* underscore that historical knowledge is dependent on memory and imagination, the two novels continue to reflect one of Muñoz Molina's primary concerns already discussed. However, whereas the narrators of the first three novels are blatantly fictional, in the following two they are such thinly disguised masks of the author that the traditional distinction between autobiography and biography (as historical genres) and their fictional novelistic counterparts is problematized. This question has already been addressed by various critics, and their work may clarify how Muñoz Molina's later novels reflect a turn towards the (auto)biographical.

Dorrit Cohn believes that the distinction between factual and fictional texts, although one subject to historical variation,[7] is an absolute one: "fiction, in short, is not a matter of degree but of kind, in first—no less than third-person form" ("Fictional *versus* Historical Lives" 16). Cohn is not alone in her insistence that there is an essential difference between factual and fictional texts. Barbara Herrnstein Smith writes that "the distinction between natural and fictive discourse is absolute" (*On the Margins* 47), and Barbara Foley agrees that "the distinction between fictional discourse and its various nonfictional counterparts—history, journalism, biography, autobiography—has remained a qualitative one" (*Telling the Truth* 27). For Philippe Lejeune, "[a]utobiography does not include degrees: it is all or nothing" (*On Autobiography* 13).

In light of the critical consensus that fiction and non-fiction are separate modes of writing, it is important to note that Lejeune qualifies his belief in the absolute difference between factual and fictional texts by admitting that "I tended to fix on an 'all or nothing' position, when in reality many intermediary positions are possible" (125). Lejeune's apparent reversal on this question springs from his original notion of an "autobiographical pact," defined by the identity of the author and the protagonist's name. Calling autobiography "a mode of reading" (30), Lejeune believes that the autobiographical pact obliges *the reader* to process the text as factual.[8] He points out that "the real reader can adopt modes of reading different from the one that is suggested to him.... [D]ifferent readings of the same text, different interpretations of the same proposed "contract" can coexist" (126). Similarly, Cohn posits that "we cannot conceive of any one given text as more or less fictional, more or less factual, but...*we read it in one key or the other*" (16; emphasis added). The importance of the reader and conventions of reading in Muñoz Molina's work should be taken into account in order to appreciate how both *El jinete polaco* and *El dueño del secreto* problematize the "all or nothing" distinction between fictional and factual narrative which Cohn and Lejeune seem to espouse—but at the same time to qualify—by referring the question to the role of the reader.

As a general rule, readers have little difficulty in deciding if a text is factual or fictional. Whether or not the author is guilty of lying or misrepresentation does not in any way alter the reader's perception of Rousseau's *Confessions* as a factual autobiography written by an author whose ontological status as a real, historical figure is unquestionable, and no reader would mistake Emily Bronte's *Jane Eyre* for a factual autobiography or Tolstoy's *The Death of Ivan Ilyitch* as the biography of a real person. However, not all texts immediately identify themselves in this way, and Cohn notes that those texts which center on a life plot occupy "the generic region where factual and fictual narratives come into closest proximity, the territory that presents the greatest potential for overlap" (Cohn 3).

As I have mentioned, for Lejeune the identity between the author's name and that of the narrator-protagonist—an "autobiographical pact"—assures the reader that the text is to be understood as a factual account of the narrator's life. This is also the case for what Lejeune calls "autobiography in the third person".[9] Following Lejeune's model, since the protagonist of *El jinete polaco* is named Manuel rather than Antonio, *El jinete polaco* is an "autobiographical novel," a fictional text

> in which the reader has reason to suspect, from the resemblances that he thinks he sees, that there is identity of author and *protagonist*, whereas the author has chosen to deny this identity, or at least not to affirm it. (*On Autobiography* 13; author's emphasis)[10]

The reader's decision to call *El jinete polaco* an "autobiographical novel" is initially problematized by one important feature: the deferral of Manuel's name until page 32. When Manuel, still unnamed, looks at the Rembrandt painting of the Polish rider and asks "[¿]Quién es[?]" (14), it is a self-conscious allusion to his own anonymity and the readers' quandary over his identity, echoed by the phrase "tampoco sabe nadie el nombre del jinete" (18). Until the narrator-protagonist is identified by name as Manuel, the text is generically ambiguous, marked by what Lejeune calls an "absent" pact (13) which does not allow the reader to opt unequivocally for either an autobiographical or a fictional reading. Even after Manuel's name has been established, a number of striking similarities between Manuel and the real author suggest a factual reading: in 1991 Manuel is the same age as Muñoz Molina was when he wrote the novel, he is raised in a town remarkably similar to the author's birthplace, Ubeda,[11] and he leaves Mágina just as Muñoz Molina left Ubeda to study in Madrid. Most importantly, Manuel's father is named Francisco and his grandmother Leonor, the real names of the author's father and grandmother on the dedicatory page.[12] *El jinete polaco* is a fictional text insofar as it uses overtly literary names (Ramiro Retratista and Nadia),[13] but since Manuel is a mask of the author, the transparency of this mask simultaneously works against the text's reading as a fiction.

El dueño del secreto takes indeterminacy one step further as the first-person narrator remains anonymous throughout and there is a total absence of Lejeune's autobiographical pact. This allows the author to pull the reader simultaneously in two opposing directions, towards a fictional and a factual reading. The text begins as a factual memoir would, with a first-person narrator and concrete temporal and spatial references: "En 1974, en Madrid, durante un par de semanas del mes de mayo, formé parte de una conspiración…" (9). Because the narrator does not identify himself and the names of streets and restaurants are verifiably real—La Gran Vía, Diego de León, Quintiliano, Lhardy, Chicote, La Mallorquina, Topic's— the text invites a factual reading. However, the names Ramón *Tovar(ich)* and *Ataúlfo* Ramiro Retamar[14] lend a distinctly literary touch, and when the narrator returns to his hometown there can be no doubt that the novel—like *El jinete polaco*—is also a fictional autobiography/memoir.[15]

The anonymous narrator of *El dueño del secreto* recalls how as a student in 1974 he became involved in a conspiracy to overthrow the Franco dictatorship. Unlike Manuel in *El jinete polaco*, the narrator does not admit to inventing a past he has never lived, and relates only what he himself has experienced directly as an eye-witness. However, *El dueño del secreto* challenges the traditional notion of history as an objective version of the past by focusing on the unreliability of the narrator's memory and on his vivid imagination.

Although the narrator of *El dueño del secreto* adopts a tone of complete sincerity, it is clear from the beginning that his memory is far from precise when he tells of the day he read about the Portuguese coup d'état of April 25, 1974: "Aún me acuerdo del momento en que leí la noticia, una tarde nublada que en mi memoria más parece de marzo" (10). Further on, he admits that "Me olvidaba de todo. La desnutrición acabó debilitándome la memoria" (21). Besides his faulty memory, the narrator also confesses that he is by no means an objective observer:

> Me he dado cuenta de que yo tiendo a magnificar las cosas nuevas que descubro y los lugares que visito por primera vez, pero ahora creo que eso no les ocurre a muchas personas. Voy a otra ciudad...y casi todo lo que veo me parece espléndido, desde los restaurantes a los paseos marítimos, y luego me entero de que la ciudad era horrible, la playa insalubre y los restaurantes vulgares y caros. (79)

The narrator does indeed "magnify things," saying that when he was hungry "[t]res personas hablando producían el fragor de una multitud. En un vagón de metro me sentía lanzado a la velocidad del sonido" (46). Excess gives an exuberantly humorous touch to many of his descriptions of characters and events. Of his roommate, Ramón, he writes, "se quedó mirando la pared sin pestañear, sin duda por ahorrarse la dosis mínima de energía requerida por el movimiento de los párpados" (14), an exaggerated depiction of sloth which recalls the story of the man who loses his sight in the carnavalesque work *El libro de buen amor*. When the narrator dines at the restaurant Lhardy, he does not spare adjectives of excess in describing one of the guests:

> De la mujer recuerdo un moño *ampuloso* y menos rubio que amarillo, unas pestañas *exageradas* y pintadas y un crucifijo de Dalí que temblaba ligeramente sobre las *amplias* blanduras pecosas del escote. (46; emphases added)

Through the use of a first-person narrator prone to exaggeration and fantasy, the events (and characters) of *El dueño del secreto* take on an unreal dimension: "Veía Madrid tras un cristal de lejanía y extrañeza enturbiado por las alucinaciones del hambre o por las borracheras instantáneas de whisky de malta" (23). The narrator also comments on how his solitude and hunger reduced him to a dream-like state in which reality and imagination became confused:

> Si entornaba los ojos durante un segundo notaba que me caía hacia adelante, y cuando volvía a abrirlos no estaba seguro de si lo que veía era real o lo estaba soñando. (49–50)
>
> El efecto del whisky se me pasaba al mismo tiempo que iba arreciando el hambre, y con ella los desvaríos febriles de la imaginación (106)
>
> Vivía...sin saber del todo si estaba despierto o dormido, si estaba soñando lo que tenía delante de mis ojos, a través del cristal escarchado de la alucinación... (112)

Muñoz Molina's "self-conscious realism"

One major tendency commented on by critics of the post-transition novel is a greater emphasis on realism. Samuel Amell has written of "a return to realism" (*Literature* 14), Rafael Conte of "un acercamiento al realismo cada vez mayor" (Amorós et al. 10), and Juan Oleza of "Realismo Abierto" or "Open Realism" (Amorós et al. 11). In 1985, Santos Alonso noted that

> Aunque desde 1976 perviven obras que continúan un intencionado experimentalismo formalista, consecuencia de los años anteriores, otras recogen, perfectamentente asumidos, sus logros estructurales para insertarlos con eficacia y equilibrio en modos narrativos diferentes. La reacción contra la complejidad experimental ha sido, de todas formas, clara y contundente. *La irrupción de un nuevo realismo* y la vuelta al lenguaje narrativo han hecho olvidar pronto el protagonismo concedido anteriormente al lenguaje discursivo. ("Un renovado compromiso" 9; emphasis added)

In 1992, when Muñoz Molina was awarded the National Prize for Literature for *El jinete polaco*, Miguel García-Posada published an article in *El País* entitled "La fuerza del nuevo realismo" in which he stated that "*El jinete polaco* supone...la vuelta franca a un nuevo realismo*" (García Posada 30). Concurring with this critic, Muñoz Molina claimed at the time that he was "hasta las narices de escribir utilizando tantos temas culturalistas" (Moret) and that "hay que optar, y he optado, por ser un escritor realista...en literatura elijo realismo" (Alameda 50). The author has also commented on his rejection of metafiction:

> [M]e sigue gustando construir bien la historia...pero el énfasis ya no lo pongo en el acto mismo de la literatura.... Eso de la metaliteratura me parece que se ha abusado de eso de una manera terrible, ¿no? Digamos que si fuera pintor, yo antes habría sido un pintor de tipo casi abstracto y que con el tiempo me voy volviendo muy figurativo. (Rich 1992)

There is evidence to support Muñoz Molina's opinion just quoted, for, prior to *El jinete polaco*, many of his reflections on writing tend to identify him as an author who views art as a product of art rather than a representation of reality, and literature as a hermetic endeavor for which the submarine Nautilus and the darkened and enclosed cinema hall are recurring metaphors:

> Sólo en las novelas y en los cines oscuros de la memoria está contenido el mundo.... No concibo otra razón para escribir. Casi nada que me importe está fuera de las novelas y los cines. Cerrado y cálido, sombrío, el mundo se contiene en ellos como en una habitación prohibida... ("Noticia de una tentativa")

> [E]l Nautilus...no es buque de guerra, sino refugio submarino contra las crudas afrentas de la realidad... (*Diario del Nautilus* 19)

In "El maleficio de los nombres," the author treats language as a means of constructing reality rather than merely reflecting it, and the article includes a semi-covert reference to one of Spain's most important modernists, Juan Ramón Jiménez, and his poem "Intelijencia:"

> Los cabalistas, que sabían, como todo el que empieza a escribir sobre un papel blanco, que el mundo fue creado por la palabra, adivinaban en ella un poderío secreto que se cifra en el nombre impronunciable de Dios. Las cosas sólo existen si las nombra una inteligencia... (*Diario del Nautilus* 39)

Nevertheless, the view that Muñoz Molina promoted of himself as a writer who had progressed chronologically from the use of anti-mimetic and metafictional modes of writing towards a greater realism is in my opinion a dangerous generalization. In fact, realism is also characteristic of his work prior to *El jinete polaco*, and despite *Beatus ille*'s metafictional conclusion, the author himself admitted that "era una novela que tenía mucho de realismo" (Rich 1992). Conversely, *El jinete polaco* and *El dueño del secreto* continue the use of intertextuality and self-reflexive strategies typical of *El invierno en Lisboa* and *Beltenebros*. I believe that the change of course towards realism which Muñoz Molina has noted not only demonstrates the frequent discrepancy between an author's theory and his/her actual practice, but also depends on a false distinction: that of metafiction vs. realism.

By affirming that he had dropped metafiction in favor of "realism," Muñoz Molina may have made the same error as some critics of contemporary fiction have—that of viewing realism and metafiction as separate and exclusive categories. Alan Wilde writes that certain American authors

> had fallen victim to an easy but inadequate habit of categorizing the fiction of the last few decades as *either* realistic *or* experimental—experimentalism being equated in this scheme simply and exclusively with metafiction... (*Middle Grounds* 3).

In fact—as I have mentioned in Chapter 2—metafiction and realism are not necessarily incompatible. Patricia Waugh states that "[m]etafiction explicitly lays bare the conventions of realism; it does not ignore or abandon them" (*Metafiction* 18), and Linda Hutcheon makes a similar point:

> what metafiction's autoreferentiality appears to do is *not* what one might expect it to, that is, to divert readers from making other references and to limit them to a narcissistic textual formalism. Instead, autoreference and intertextual reference actually combine to direct readers back to an outer reference; in fact, they direct the readers outside the text... ("Metafictional" 10)

If one accepts that metafiction and realism are not mutually exclusive categories, one is in a better position to appreciate the character not only of Muñoz Molina's work, but that of other contemporary Spanish novelists. Joan Lipman Brown writes that Carmen Martín Gaite's metafiction *El cuarto de atrás* "encompasses two very distinct genres. It is a fantastic novel, while at the same time it is a realistic memoir" ("Fantastic Memoir" 13), and Diane Garvey refers to Juan Marsé's *Si te dicen que caí* as "at once self-reflexive and a reflection of an historical period" ("Juan Marsé's" 376).[16] Like Martín Gaite and Marsé, Muñoz Molina could be said to be practising a "self-conscious realism" in which metafictional strategies do not exclude the use of concrete historical references. Viewed in this way, *El jinete polaco*, contrary to what the author himself has proposed, would not represent so radical a break with Muñoz Molina's previous novels. While it is true that *El jinete polaco* is "realistic" insofar as its fictional world (what Benjamin Harshaw calls its "internal frame of reference") is anchored firmly in the external reality of Spanish history, it is simultaneously a metafiction in which Manuel functions as a "visibly inventing narrator" (Waugh 21) who says "Puedo inventar ahora...uno o dos recuerdos falsos pero no inverosímiles..." (193). Similarly, although *El dueño del secreto* is not an explicitly metafictional text, the literary names of its characters and its unreliable narrator self-consciously undermine its status as a historically verisimilar memoir.

In his book *La novela en la transición (1976–1981)*, after noting that a characteristic of the post-transition novel is "una tendencia hacia el realismo," Santos Alonso writes:

> El afirmar que la forma novelesca característica de la transición es, por consiguiente, la realista puede suponer...una paradoja.... La contradicción sería en todo caso sólo en apariencia: los extremos han sido más formales que materiales. Si analizamos, por ejemplo, las novelas-hito del franquismo, llegaremos a esta conclusión: el cambio producido...es fundamentalmente formal; *el tono, la ambientación, los personajes, etc. son realistas*; las formas de expresión, los procedimientos, y las técnicas pueden ser, y lo son de hecho, distintos. (59; emphasis added)

Muñoz Molina's "self-conscious realism" exemplifies the apparent contradiction which Santos Alonso has noted between formal innovation and traditional realist techniques. *El jinete polaco* and *El dueño del secreto* may be metafictions, but they are also realistic—to use Santos Alonso's words—in "el tono, la ambientación, los personajes."

Notes

[1] The author himself has referred to *El jinete polaco* as both "una ficción autobiográfica" (see note 10) and as a biography: "Podría definirse como biográfica" (Gómez 122). The novel alternates between first- and third-person narration, a strategy to which the narrator self-consciously refers: "Ya no soy quien fui, y por eso puedo hablar de mí mismo en tercera persona..." (*El jinete polaco* 535).

[2] "Yo quería contar una historia familiar en un pueblo pequeño, con padres e hijos, pero siempre que me ponía se me iba la mano y me salía una novela suramericana. He estado años con ese problema, ya que la empecé a los 19" (Moret 35). Grandfather Manuel's wife scolds him for telling fantastic tales (81–82), which offers a striking parallel to Ursula and José Arcadio Buendía in *Cien años de soledad*.

[3] In an interview, Muñoz Molina said that "En los libros siempre se cuenta uno a sí mismo" (Alameda 50).

[4] *El País semanal* 7 May 1989: n. pag.

[5] "[P]articipó en una manifestación por la muerte del anarquista Puig Antich, en 1974, y resultó detenido y llevado a la Dirección General de Seguridad. Le pegaron, luego le soltaron y le pusieron 'un multón enorme' de 5.000 pesetas... 'La experiencia de la detención, contada en *Beatus Ille*, me dejó tal miedo en el corazón que no podía hacer nada'" (Sorela 18).

[6] See notes 16 and 17 to Chapter 2. In *La realidad de la ficción*, Muñoz Molina writes that his short story "La poseída" was based on a personal experience, and the protagonist's name, Marino, provides another example of the author disguising his name. I have analyzed in greater detail the significance of names in an unpublished article, "Dobles y espejos: La función poética de los nombres en *Beatus ille* y *Beltenebros* de Antonio Muñoz Molina," which was presented at the Sixth Biennial Northeast Regional Meeting of the AATSP in New Haven on October 1, 1994.

[7] "[T]he boundaries between fiction and nonfiction, between literature and nonliterature and so forth are not laid up in heaven. Every specific situation is historical" (Bakhtin 33).

[8] "The history of autobiography would be therefore, above all, a history of its mode of reading" (*On Autobiography* 30).

9 See Lejeune's essay "Autobiography in the Third Person" in chapter 2 of *On Autobiography*.

10 Echoing Lejeune's theoretical position, Muñoz Molina called *El jinete polaco* "una ficción autobiográfica." ("Antonio Muñoz Molina gana el Planeta con 'una ficción en forma autobiográfica'." *El País* 16 October, 1991: n. pag.)

11 See Muñoz Molina's article "Mágina. La ciudad inventada," in which he writes "la Ubeda arcaica y campesina de mi infancia y la Mágina de mis libros se me vuelven idénticas" (58).

12 The dedicatory page reads "Para Antonia Molina Expósito y Francisco Muñoz Valenzuela. Para Leonor Expósito Medina, *in memoriam*. Dedications are by definition extrafictional structures— which Gérard Genette calls "paratexts."

13 Referring to Jules Verne's novel *Michel Strogoff*, Muñoz Molina revealed that "el nombre del personaje femenino, Nadia, procede de la novia de Strogoff, que se llamaba así" (Rodríguez, Emma 36).

14 "Tovarich" is "comrade" in Russian. The name humorously reinforces the character's commitment to revolutionary ideals. "Ataúlfo" was a Visigothic king who reigned in Spain from 410 to 415 A.D. His second surname "Retamar" is also that of the Cuban pro-Castro critic Roberto Fernández Retamar.

15 I use a slash between autobiography and memoir because there is no clearly defined limit between the two forms. As Lejeune writes of autobiography, "The subject must be *primarily* individual life, the genesis of the personality; but the chronicle and social or political history can also be part of the narrative. It is a question here of proportion, or rather of hierarchy: some transitions with other genres of personal literature work quite naturally (memoirs, diary, essay), and a certain latitude is left to the classifier in the examination of particular cases" (*On Autobiography* 5; author's emphasis).

16 In *Beatus ille*, Manuel shows Minaya Solana's room, saying "Ahí tienes...la ventana y el espejo de los que habla ese poema" (28). In my opinion, the window and the mirror represent the tension between mimesis and self-reflexivity that characterizes Muñoz Molina's narrative.

Conclusion

"El Desencanto"

Contrary to what might have been expected, the death of Franco in 1975 and Spain's subsequent transition to a democratic regime did not automatically eliminate the deeply rooted historical differences between supporters of the left (Republicans) and the right (Nationalists), for as late as 1987, "undercurrents of resentment and tensions emanating from the war years [were] still present in large sectors of Spanish society" (López Guerra 256). According to Luis López Guerra, the forging of a political consensus necessary to effect a peaceful transition depended on suppressing Spain's past, because no political group—including the Socialists who eventually won the 1982 elections—wished to revive painful memories of the Civil War and Francoism:

> We must not forget that the transition to democracy in Spain was founded on a compromise between the inheritors of General Franco's policies and representatives of the opposition, all of whom agreed to forget past controversies and sometimes even their own biographies prior to 1977. (López Guerra 246)

However, unlike the politicians who attempted to eliminate memories of Spain's conflictive past in order to facilitate the political transition, Muñoz Molina has been committed to keeping these memories alive:

> Yo creo que el presente contiene todos los instantes del pasado y a mí me gusta buscar las partes del pasado que, por ser raíces del presente, están todavía vivas, y reivindicar esa zona del pasado español obligatoriamente negada. (Rodríguez, Juan María, n. pag.)

For Muñoz Molina, that part of Spain's past which has been "obligatorily denied" by most politicians of the post-transition period represented the only hope for Spain's political, economic, and cultural regeneration.

When he was asked why he had chosen a poet of the Generation of '27 as the protagonist of *Beatus ille*, the author answered:

> Ese momento, como ha señalado Juan Marichal, es el de la universalización de España, cuando estuvo a punto de convertirse en una patria para todos los españoles. Esa esperanza fue abolida por la guerra civil, y es la gran tragedia nacional. Es un episodio fundamental de nuestra experiencia personal y colectiva.... Su valor sigue siendo absoluto porque representa a la mejor tradición, verdaderamente democrática, estética, civil y política, que tenemos. (Gutiérrez n. pag.)

In Muñoz Molina's opinion, the political transition and the victory of the Spanish Socialist Workers Party (PSOE) in 1982 offered a second opportunity for Spain's regeneration, but one which again was not seized:

> Ahora, la izquierda que hace la democracia no hace la democracia, sino que es admitida al juego de la democracia instaurada por los herederos de la dictadura. Esa izquierda, en vez de reivindicar lo mejor de su propia tradición, lo que hace es asumir la indignidad moral de la dictadura. Y jugamos en ese campo de indignidad moral. (Ribas 52)

The term "desencanto" has been used to describe the sense of disillusionment which characterizes many members of a generation of Spaniards who have—to some degree or another—lost faith in the progressive political and social ideals of their youth. It also reflects the reaction of Spaniards who, like Muñoz Molina, have seen the destructive by-products of economic "progress" since Franco's death. This is voiced by Manuel in *El jinete polaco* as he returns to Mágina:

> las calles sucias, intransitables por el tráfico, los caminos del campo cegados por el abandono y la basura, frigoríficos viejos y lavadoras y televisores rotos en astillas, cristales de botellas, envoltorios desgarrados de plástico, una epidemia de zafiedad y de mugre... (545)

Similarly, *Los misterios de Madrid* depicts the urban blight that Quesada encounters in a Madrid full of criminals, prostitutes, and drug addicts, a condemnation of the inability of the PSOE to eliminate the savage economic inequalities which Francoism had left in its wake. *Los misterios de Madrid* also contains an ironic critique of the continuing residue of Francoist ideology in rural areas: Quesada and the narrator are inhabitants of a small town which values a religious image more than its cultural and social development. And although Quesada—through the narrator—speaks disparagingly of "las provincias más incultas" (7), he in fact embodies the cultural backwardness that characterized Spain under Francoism, referring to El Greco as "ese pintor que hacía los santos alargados por culpa de un defecto de la vista" (16) and believing that "la raza amarilla está empezando a dominar el mundo" (30).

"El desencanto" also reflects the difficulty of overcoming the ingrained pessimism instilled in Muñoz Molina's generation by years of Francoism. This is evident in *El jinete polaco*, in which Manuel's family and friends are seen as suffering psychologically from the effects of the Franco dictatorship, their solitude and fear depicted as historically determined and collectively inherited traits. The members of Manuel's generation are

> habitados hasta la médula de su conciencia por las voces de sus mayores, herederos de un valor fracasado mucho antes de que nacieran y modelados sin saberlo por hechos memorables o atroces de los que nada sabían, herederos involuntarios de la soledad, del sufrimiento y del amor de quienes los habían engendrado. (12)

Manuel later remarks:

> No sólo repetíamos las canciones y los juegos de nuestros mayores y estábamos condenados a repetir sus vidas: nuestras imaginaciones y nuestras palabras repetían el miedo que fue suyo y que sin premeditación nos transmitieron desde que nacimos… (46)

Throughout this study, my hypothesis has been that Muñoz Molina's work is an expression of Spain's "desencanto," not only on the level of theme and content, but also on the level of form and structure. The implication is that his technical strategies—including his generic parodies and historiographic metafictions—must not be viewed simply as abstract experiments or *divertissements*, but rather as sources of contemporary social commentary. This can best be appreciated if one considers the moral-epistemological crisis which underlies "el desencanto." Muñoz Molina uses metafiction to deconstruct conventional notions of historical knowledge, and by doing so discredits the dogmatic versions of the Civil War in which both the left and the right have so long believed. Although the implied author of his novels is evidently anti-Francoist, he consistently challenges the left's idealization of the heroic anti-Franco militant. I have discussed in detail the demythicizing of Solana and Darman in chapter 2, and Commander Galaz in *El jinete polaco* provides yet another example. Mágina remembers Galaz as a hero for having shot Lieutenant Mestalla and for having impeded the defection of the town's army to the side of

Franco's rebel forces. Galaz has attained the status of myth: the child Manuel describes him as "una figura imaginaria y poderosa…tan mitológica como Don Manuel Azaña o como el general de bronce que había en la plaza del Reloj" (*El jinete* 156). However, the townspeople of Mágina are not aware that Galaz "carecía tan absolutamente de vocación militar como de cualquier otra vocación imaginable" (238), nor that "[n]o había elegido arrebatadamente una causa, no lo habían cegado ni la pasión política, que le era indiferente, ni una voluntad de heroísmo heredada de sus mayores…" (219). As in the case of Solana, Galaz's fame is a consequence of the political left's quasi-religious need to add another "saint" to its pantheon of militant heros. In fact, he is simply another "desencantado."

By blurring the boundaries between fiction and reality, Muñoz Molina's metafictions serve to undermine the foundations of empirical epistemology: reality is no longer a stable concept, and history becomes confused with myth. Epistemological uncertainty leads to moral ambiguity, for—as *Beltenebros* demonstrates with its doubles Darman and Andrade—when events are never clarified, there is no ultimate authority that can distinguish heroism from treason.

Muñoz Molina rejects the politically committed literature of neorealism. In "Decadencia del crimen," he writes that "el crimen político es tan detestable como el arte social" (*Diario del Nautilus* 118), and he once remarked: "no me gustan los intelectuales comprometidos tipo Sartre" (Moreno 345). In a 1988 interview, although denying that the authors of his generation shared any common literary characteristics, he added:

> Sí hay, desde luego, un hecho sociológico concreto: quienes rondamos ahora los 30 años nos hemos educado en un amor a la literatura bastante virulento, en un amor apasionado por la ficción, por el placer de contar historias despojadas de cualquier compromiso moral y político. (Solana VI)

Nevertheless, while appearing to reject the view of literature as a vehicle for explicit moral or political commitment, Muñoz Molina has also acknowledged the moral import of fiction. In his article "La edad de la novela," he wrote that "toda novela memorable contiene una severa afirmación moral," and in an interview stated: "Yo no creo en ese compromiso político militante en que se creía antes, ahora lo que sí creo es que hay una especie de responsabilidad moral en el escritor (Gopegui 116). This ambivalent attitude is also characteristic of authors who were adolescents during the post-war period:

> [E]stos novelistas…se despojan de todo compromiso político, pero sin olvidar en ningún momento las circunstancias generacionales, lo cual les lleva a realizar una visión crítica de la realidad española a través de la propia memoria o de la memoria común… (Alonso, "Novelistas de los 70" 26)

Muñoz Molina's texts dramatize the ethical dilemma posed by Spain's post-transition "desencanto:" the problem of how the members of a society that has steadily lost faith in utopian leftist ideals can possibly find values with which to replace them. The author's work to date show characters who can find no solution to their *malaise*, a phenomenon which Santos Sanz Villanueva has commented on as characteristic of Muñoz Molina's immediate predecessors:

> [es] como si las promociones de posguerra no hubieran encontrado un sentido satisfactorio a sus existencias, ni hubieran sido capaces de ofrecer un sugestivo proyecto colectivo. ("Una realidad" 4).

Faced with this dilemma, Muñoz Molina has suggested that one can only resort to individual solutions:

> La idea ilustrada del imperio de la ley ya no existe; ahora hay otro monstruo: la inseguridad absoluta, que *te lleva a buscar protecciones privadas*…. El recurso es el de la moral del detective privado: en el ámbito en que uno se mueve, afirmar la moral, la ternura y la solidaridad, así como en el ámbito del trabajo, pues hacer bien algo te sitúa en el lugar de los justos, de los que salvan su generación. (Cruz 32; emphasis added)

It is therefore not surprising that Muñoz Molina has adopted the *novela negra* as one of his primary intertexts, using this genre to portray the isolation of the individual in a society where—in the words of a popular expression—"heroism is dead," and ethical choices have lost almost any collective significance.

Testifying to that lack of a "proyecto colectivo" to which Sanz Villanueva has referred, Muñoz Molina's characters are consistently depicted as solitary anti-heroes forced to live on the margins of society, adrift in a world from which they feel permanently alienated.[1] They either die in isolation (Solana), disappear (Biralbo), live as exiles[2] (Darman, Comandante Galaz), or end up engulfed in the mediocrity of small-town life (Quesada, Funes, the anonymous narrator of *El dueño del secreto*). Caught between an intolerable present and a tragic past, these characters are mirrors of Spain's "desencantados," who can only find solace in either nostalgia or romantic fantasies. The narrator of *El dueño del secreto* reflects that "[n]adie sabe que aún continúo añorando lo que no sucedió nunca, la revolución franca y gozosa que no llegó a triunfar..." (146) and ends by wistfully reminiscing about an aborted erotic encounter which he describes as "una de tantas puertas que se cierran para no abrirse más en la vida de uno" (148). Nostalgia—as the nineteenth-century romantics discovered—is never a permanent solution to an individual's disconformity with the present, and Muñoz Molina must have sensed this when he reacted defensively to an interviewer who had commented on the nostalgic element in *El jinete polaco*. The author replied: "no es una nostalgia blanda, sino confrontada con los hechos. Yo, más que de nostalgia, hablaría de fidelidad, de agradecimiento hacia su pasado" (Pita).

At the end of *Ardor guerrero*, the author-narrator telephones Pepe, a friend he had met during his military service, only to learn that Pepe had died some time ago in a car accident, "borrado por la muerte, entre un desastre de vidrios rotos y metales machacados" (384). The text concludes with a self-reflexive comment: "La ventaja de la ficción es que no tolera finales tan innobles" (384). It has often been said that fiction has a therapeutic effect, offering psychological solace to those who wish to shield themselves from a hostile and often inexplicable world. Thus it is significant—and ironic—that the final sentence of *Ardor guerrero* is a eulogy to the capacity of fiction to create imaginary and ideal worlds, but occurs in a text that purports to be a non-fictional memoir. As an expression of Spain's "desencanto," Muñoz Molina's self-conscious realism might best be described as fiction which is inherently paradoxical, insofar as it uses the confluence of memory and imagination to simultaneously capture and flee from the reality of Spain's past and present. The tension between the real and the imaginary which manifests itself throughout Muñoz Molina's work was best summed up by the author himself:

> La literatura es...una incruenta conjura no en favor de los sueños y en contra de la vida, sino de un modo de vivir en el que la realidad y el deseo se afirman mutuamente y en el que el derecho y el privilegio de la huida se corresponde con el don siempre misterioso del reconocimiento y la aproximación. (*La realidad de la ficción* 80–81)

Notes

1. Muñoz Molina often uses the term "náufrago" to describe his characters: his Urban Robinson is "[n]áufrago y desdeñado" (*El Robinson urbano* 25); Manuel and those living with him are "[n]áufragos" (*Beatus ille* 65); Rebeca and Walter are "dos náufragos...condenados a vivir para siempre en una costa abandonada" (*Beltenebros* 115); Ramiro Retratista is a "náufrago tardío en Madrid" (*El jinete polaco* 60).

2. Maraña, who aids Biralbo in getting a false passport, is described as a political exile (*El invierno en Lisboa* 176), and Biralbo identifies himself with Maraña as he ponders "¿no era también él, Biralbo, un desterrado, no había tenido que irse al extranjero para triunfar en la música?" (176). While *El invierno en Lisboa* is not a text with an explicitly historical theme, the reference to Biralbo as an artistic exile evokes an entire generation of artists and writers—including Rafael Alberti, Luis Buñuel and Pablo Picasso—who either had to leave Spain or remain as part of the "exilio interior," with their work often censored by the Franco regime. For an excellent bibliography of works on the subject of the Spanish exile, see Naharro-Calderón (427–459). Paul Ilie's *Literatura y exilio interior* offers a discussion of the "exilio interior," a concept which Naharro-Calderón critiques. One of the major psychological effects of exile is an intense feeling of solitude, which not surprisingly is a trait of all Muñoz Molina's characters. As the narrator says of Biralbo and Lucrecia, "cada uno de ellos seguía estando infinitamente solo, condenado y perdido" (78). "Soledad" and "solo" are used to describe Minaya (*Beatus ille* 16, 17), Manuel (24), Solana (8, 124), Doña Elvira (70), the anonymous narrator of *El invierno en Lisboa* (11), Biralbo (16, 17), Malcolm (131), Lucrecia (186), Darman (*Beltenebros* 33), Andrade (84) and Rebeca (221). References to solitude in *El jinete polaco* are too numerous to mention, recalling one of its primary intertexts, *Cien años de soledad*.

BIBLIOGRAPHY

Abrams, M. H. *The Mirror and the Lamp: Romantic Theory and the Critical Tradition.* Oxford University Press, 1971.

Alameda, Soledad. "Un hijo de la España profunda." *El País semanal* 8 Dec. 1991: 48–54.

Alonso, Santos. *La novela en la transición* (1976–1981). Madrid: Dante, 1983.

——. "Novelistas de los 70." *Doce años de cultura española (1976–1987).* Ed. Equipo Reseña. Madrid: Ediciones Encuentro, 1989. 25–32.

——. "Un renovado compromiso con el realismo y con el hombre." *Insula* 464–465 (1985): 9–10.

Alter, Robert. *Partial Magic. The Novel as a Self-Conscious Genre.* Berkeley: University of California Press, 1975.

Amell, Samuel, ed. *Literature, the Arts, and Democracy. Spain in the Eighties.* Trans. Alma Amell. London and Toronto: Associated University Presses, 1990.

——. "La novela negra y los narradores españoles actuales." *Revista de estudios hispánicos* 20.1 (1986): 91–102.

Amorós, Andrés, et al. "El estado de la cuestión. Novela española 1989–1990." *Insula* 525 (1990): 9–23.

Arias, Jesús. "Muñoz Molina, en el cine." *El País* (Barcelona) 30 Sep. (1989): 37.

Azancot, Leopoldo. "*El invierno en Lisboa.*" *ABC* 30 May 1987: n. pag.

Azancot, Nuria. "Muñoz Molina: 'Un buen escritor expresa el presente, porque lo lleva dentro'." *ABC* 13 July, 1988: n. pag.

Bakhtin, Mikhail. *The Dialogic Imagination. Four Essays by M. M. Bakhtin.* Ed. Michael Holquist. Trans. Caryl Emerson and Michael Holquist. Austin: The University of Texas Press, 1981.

Barth, John. "The Literature of Exhaustion." *The Atlantic* 220.2 (1967): 29–34.

Barthes, Roland. "The Death of the Author." *Image, Music, Text*. Trans. Stephen Heath. New York: The Noonday Press, 1988. 142–148.

——. "An Introduction to the Structural Analysis of Narrative." *New Literary History* 6 (1975): 237–72.

——. *S/Z*. Trans. Richard Miller. New York: Hill and Wang, 1974.

Baudelaire, Charles. *Obra completa en poesía*. Edición Bilingüe. Trans. Enrique Parellada. Barcelona: Ediciones 29, 1984.

Benveniste, Emile. "The Correlations of Tense in the French Verb." *Problems in General Linguistics*. Trans. Mary Elizabeth Meek. Coral Gables: University of Miami Press, 1971. 205–15.

Bértolo, Constantino. "El melodrama en negro." *El País* Sección Libros 5 March 1989: 15.

Booth, Wayne C. *The Rhetoric of Fiction*. Chicago and London: The University of Chicago Press, 1961.

Borges, Jorge Luis. *Ficciones*. 2nd ed. Barcelona: Seix Barral, 1986.

Brown, Joan Lipman. "A Fantastic Memoir: Technique and History in *El cuarto de atrás*." *Anales de la literatura española contemporánea* 6 (1981): 13–20.

Cantavella, Juan. "Antonio Muñoz Molina: 'El que no entra en la literatura por amor a ella se equivoca.'" *Ideal* (Granada) 9 March 1989: n. pag.

Cawelti, John G. *Adventure, Mystery, and Romance: Formula Stories as Art and Popular Culture*. Chicago and London: University of Chicago Press, 1976.

Cervantes, Miguel de. *Don Quijote de la Mancha*. Ed. Martín de Riquer. Barcelona: Planeta, 1980.

Cohn, Dorrit. "Fictional *versus* Historical Lives: Borderlines and Borderline Cases." *The Journal of Narrative Technique* 19.1 (1989): 3–24.

Coleridge, Samuel. *Biographia Literaria*. Ed. George Watson. London: J. M. Dent & Sons, 1991.

Compitello, Malcolm Alan. "Benet and Spanish Postmodernism." *Revista Hispánica Moderna* XLIV (1991): 259–73.

Conte, Rafael. "*El jinete polaco.*" *ABC literario* 8 Nov. 1991: 7.

Cortázar, Julio. *Rayuela*. Barcelona: Seix Barral, 1984.

Cruz, Juan and Juan Arias. "Hay que reducir el infierno." *El País* 8 June 1992: 32–33.

Culler, Jonathan. *On Deconstruction. Theory and Criticism After Structuralism*. Ithaca: Cornell University Press, 1982.

———. *The Pursuit of Signs. Semiotics, Literature, Deconstruction*. Ithaca: Cornell University Press, 1981.

———. *Structuralist Poetics. Structuralism, Linguistics and the Study of Literature*. Ithaca: Cornell University Press, 1975.

Dove, George N. "The Detection Formula and the Act of Reading." *The Cunning Craft. Original Essays on Detective Fiction and Contemporary Literary Theory*. Ed. Ronald G. Walker and June M. Frazer. Western Illinois University, 1990. 25–37.

Durán, Manuel. "Fiction and Metafiction in Contemporary Spanish Letters." *World Literature Today* 60.3 (1986): 398–402.

Eco, Umberto. "Postmodernism, Irony, the Enjoyable." *Postscript to "The Name of the Rose"*. Trans. William Weaver. San Diego, New York and London: Harcourt Brace Jovanovich, 1984. 65–72.

Eliot, T. S. "Wordsworth and Coleridge." *The Use of Poetry and the Use of Criticism. Studies in the Relation of Criticism to Poetry in England*. 2nd ed. London: Faber and Faber, 1964. 67–85.

Faulkner, William. *Absalom, Absalom!* New York: Vintage, 1972.

Foley, Barbara. *Telling the Truth. The Theory and Practice of Documentary Fiction*. Ithaca and London: Cornell University Press, 1986.

Foucault, Michel. *The Archaeology of Knowledge and the Discourse on Language*. Trans. A. M. Sheridan Smith. New York: Pantheon, 1972.

Freund, Elizabeth. *The Return of the Reader. Reader-Response Criticism*. London and New York: Methuen, 1987.

Frow, John. "Intertextuality and Ontology." *Intertextuality: Theories and Practices*. Ed. Michael Worton and Judith Still. Manchester: Manchester University Press, 1990. 45–55.

García, Angeles. "No somos huérfanos ideológicos del Mayo Francés." *El País* 25–26 Dec. 1991: 26.

García Márquez, Gabriel. *Cien años de soledad.* Barcelona: Edhasa, 1969.

García-Moreno Barco, Francisco. *La narrativa española de los 80 a la luz de la crítica posmodernista: El caso de Antonio Muñoz Molina.* Diss. Michigan State University, 1992. Ann Arbor: UMI, 1992. 9302996.

García-Posada, Miguel. "La fuerza del nuevo realismo." El País 6 June 1992: 30.

Garvey, Diane I. "Juan Marsé's *Si te dicen que caí*: The Self-reflexive Text and the Question of Referentiality." *Modern Language Notes* 95 (1980): 376–87.

Genette, Gérard. *Narrative Discourse. An Essay in Method.* Trans. Jane E. Lewin. Ithaca, New York: Cornell University Press, 1980.

———. *Narrative Discourse Revisited.* Ithaca: Cornell University Press, 1988.

Gombrich, E. H. "Representation and Misrepresentation." *Critical Inquiry* 11.2 (1984): 195–201.

Gómez, Juan Enrique. "Entrevista. Antonio Muñoz Molina." *Tribuna* 21 Oct. 1991: 122–23.

Gopegui, Belén. "Entrevista. Antonio Muñoz Molina." *Tribuna* 19–25 June 1989: 116–17.

Goytisolo, Juan. *Disidencias.* Barcelona: Seix Barral, 1977.

Grella, George. "Murder and Manners: The Formal Detective Novel." *Dimensions of Detective Fiction.* Ed. Larry N. Landrum et al. Bowling Green: Bowling Green University Popular Press, 1976. 37–57.

———. "The Hard-Boiled Detective Novel." *Detective Fiction. A Collection of Critical Essays.* Ed. Robin W. Winks. Woodstock: The Countryman Press, 1988. 103–20.

Gutiérrez, José. "Mi novela es una historia de amor." Ideal (Granada) 22 Dec. 1986: n. pag.

Harshaw (Hrushovski), Benjamin. "Fictionality and Fields of Reference. Remarks on a Theoretical Framework." *Poetics Today.* 5.2 (1984): 227–51.

Hart, Patricia. *The Spanish Sleuth. The Detective in Spanish Fiction.* London and Toronto: Associated University Presses, 1987.

Herzberger, David K. "Metafiction and the Contemporary Spanish Novel." *Selected Proceedings. 32nd Mountain Interstate Foreign Language Conference.* Ed. Gregorio C. Martín. Winston-Salem: Wake Forest University, 1984. 145–52.

——. "Narrating the Past: History and the Novel of Memory in Postwar Spain." *Publications of the Modern Language Association of America* 106.1 (1991): 34–45.

Higham, Charles and Joel Greenberg. *Hollywood in the Forties.* New York: A. S. Barnes, 1968.

Hornung, Alfred. "Reading One/Self. Samuel Beckett, Thomas Bernhard, Peter Handke, John Barth, Alain Robbe-Grillet." *Exploring Postmodernism. Selected papers presented at the XIth International Comparative Literature Congress, Paris, 20–24 August 1985.* Ed. Matei Calinescu and Douwe Fokkema. Amsterdam and Philadelphia: John Benjamins Publishing Company, 1987. 175–98.

Hühn, Peter. "The Detective as Reader: Narrativity and Reading Concepts in Detective Fiction." *Modern Fiction Studies* 33.3 (1987): 451–66.

Hutcheon, Linda. "Literary Borrowing...and Stealing: Plagiarism, Sources, Influences, and Intertexts." *English Studies in Canada* 12.2 (1986): 229–39.

——. "Metafictional Implications for Novelistic Reference." *On Referring in Literature.* Ed. Anna Whiteside and Michael Issacharoff. Bloomington and Indianapolis: Indiana University Press, 1987. 1–13.

——. *Narcissistic Narrative. The Metafictional Paradox.* London: Routledge, 1991.

——. *A Poetics of Postmodernism. History, Theory, Fiction.* New York: Routledge, 1988.

Hyslop, Lois Boe. *Charles Baudelaire Revisited.* New York: Twayne, 1992.

Ilie, Paul. *Literatura y exilio interior. Escritores y sociedad en la España franquista.* Madrid: Fundamentos, 1981.

Iser, Wolfgang. *The Act of Reading. A Theory of Aesthetic Response.* Baltimore and London: The Johns Hopkins University Press, 1978.

——. *The Implied Reader. Patterns of Communication in Prose Fiction from Bunyan to Beckett.* Baltimore and London: The Johns Hopkins University Press, 1974.

——. "Indeterminacy and the Reader's Response in Prose Fiction." *Aspects of Narrative. Selected Papers from the English Institute.* Ed. J. Hillis Miller. New York and London: Columbia University Press, 1971. 1–45.

Jakobson, Roman. *Language in Literature*. Ed. Krystyna Pomorska and Stephen Rudy. Cambridge and London: Belknap Press of Harvard University Press, 1987.

——. "Linguistics and Poetics." *Style in Language*. Ed. Thomas A. Sebeok. Cambridge: MIT Press, 1960. 350–77.

——. "On Realism in Art." *Language in Literature*. Ed. Krystyna Pomorska and Stephen Rudy. Cambridge and London: Belknap Press of Harvard University Press, 1987. 19–27.

—— and Claude Lévi-Strauss. "Baudelaire's 'Les Chats'." *Language in Literature*. 180–97.

Jauss, Hans Robert. "Literary History as a Challenge to Literary Theory." *New Directions in Literary History*. Ed. Ralph Cohen. Baltimore: The Johns Hopkins University Press, 1974. 11–41.

Joyce, James. *Ulysses*. New York: Vintage, 1961.

Kadir, Djelal. *Juan Carlos Onetti*. Boston: Twayne, 1977.

Krieger, Murray. "The Ambiguities of Representation and Illusion: An E. H. Gombrich Retrospective." *Critical Inquiry* 11.2 (1984): 181–94.

Kristeva, Julia. "Word Dialogue and Novel." *The Kristeva Reader*. Ed. Toril Moi. Oxford: Basil Blackwell, 1986. 34–61.

Labanyi, Jo. *Myth and History in the Contemporary Spanish Novel*. New York: Cambridge University Press, 1989.

Lanser, Susan Sniader. *The Narrative Act. Point of View in Prose Fiction*. Princeton: Princeton University Press, 1981.

Larra, Mariano José de. *Artículos varios*. Madrid: Castalia, 1986.

Lejeune, Philippe. *On Autobiography*. Ed. Paul John Eakin. Trans. Katherine Leary. Minneapolis: University of Minnesota Press, 1989.

Llamazares, Julio. *Luna de lobos*. 10th ed. Barcelona: Seix Barral, 1989.

Lodge, David. *After Bakhtin. Essays on fiction and criticism*. London and New York: Routledge, 1990. 143–53.

López Guerra, Luis. "The Legacy of the Spanish Civil War Today." *Rewriting the Good Fight. Critical Essays on the Literature of the Spanish Civil War*. Ed. Frieda S. Brown et al. East Lansing: Michigan State University Press, 1989. 243–59.

Mainer, José-Carlos. *La Edad de Plata (1902–1939). Ensayo de interpretación de un proceso cultural.* 4th ed. Madrid: Cátedra, 1987.

———. "1975–1985: The Powers of the Past." *Literature, the Arts, and Democracy. Spain in the Eighties.* Ed. Samuel Amell. Trans. Alma Amell. London and Toronto: Associated University Presses, 1990. 16–37.

Marco, Joaquín. *"Nada del otro mundo." ABC literario* n.d. n. pag.

Martín Gil, Juan Francisco. "El que habita en la oscuridad." *Quimera* 83 (1988): 24–29.

McHale, Brian. *Postmodernist Fiction.* London and New York: Routledge, 1987.

Michael, Ian. "From Scarlet Study to Novela Negra. The Detective Story in Spanish." *Leeds Papers on Thrillers in Transition. "Novela negra" and Political Change in Spain.* Ed. Rob Rix. Trinity and All Saints College, 1992. 17–47.

Montesinos, José F. *Costumbrismo y novela. Ensayo sobre el redescubrimiento de la realidad española.* Berkeley and Los Angeles: University of California Press, 1960.

Morales Cuesta, Manuel María. *La voz narrativa de Antonio Muñoz Molina.* Barcelona: Octaedro, 1996.

Moreno, Sebastián. "Un escritor en plenitud. Antonio Muñoz Molina." *Tiempo* (Suplemento) 24 Feb. 1992: 344–45.

Moret, Xavier. "Antonio Muñoz Molina. Novelista ganador del Planeta." *El País* 17 Oct. 1991: 35.

Muñoz Molina, Antonio. *Ardor guerrero.* Madrid: Alfaguara, 1995.

———. "Arte nuevo de escribir novelas." *El País* 25 Nov. 1987: 13–14.

———. *Beatus Ille.* 4th ed. Barcelona: Seix Barral, 1990.

———. *Beltenebros.* México: Editorial Planeta Mexicana, 1990.

———. "Byron, the wanderer." *ABC literario* 23 Jan. 1988: XV.

———. "La cara del pasado." *El País* 8 Feb. (1990): 13.

———. *Córdoba de los omeyas.* Barcelona: Planeta, 1991.

———. "Correspondencia." *ABC literario* 7 Nov. 1987: XVI.

———. "Cuando Onetti." *ABC literario* 5 Dec. 1987: XVI.

———. "Desocupado lector." *ABC literario* 26 March 1988: XVI.

——. "El detective inexistente." *ABC literario* 3 Sep. 1988: XVI.

——. "Los detectives." *El País* 12 June 1992: 42.

——. *Diario del Nautilus*. Madrid: Mondadori, 1989.

——. *El dueño del secreto*. Madrid: Ollero & Ramos, 1994.

——. "La edad de la novela." *ABC literario* 16 April 1988: VIII.

——. "Fábula de Fuentes. *ABC* 21 April 1988: n. pag.

——. *El invierno en Lisboa*. 19th ed. Barcelona: Seix Barral, 1990.

——. *El jinete polaco*. Barcelona: Planeta, 1991.

——. "Lecciones de abismo." *ABC* 17 April 1988: 64.

——. "Lectura y adicción". *ABC literario*. 20 Aug. 1988: XII.

——. "Los libros y los trenes." *ABC literario* 21 Jan. 1989: XVI.

——. "Un lugar donde vivir." *ABC literario* 21 May 1988: XVI.

——. "Mágina. La ciudad inventada." *El País semanal* 14 Aug. 1994: 50–59.

——. "La manera de vivir." *El País* 17 Feb. 1990: 29.

——. "La mano de nieve." *ABC literario* 21 Nov. 1987: XVI.

——. "Los mantequeros de Perú." *El País* 26 May 1990: 34.

——. "Las máquinas del tiempo." *ABC literario* 18 Feb. 1989: XVI.

——. "La mirada que pinta." *ABC literario* 20 May 1989: XVI.

——. *Los misterios de Madrid*. Barcelona: Seix Barral, 1992.

——. *Nada del otro mundo*. Madrid: Espasa Calpe, 1993.

——. "Noticia de una tentativa." *El País* 29 May 1986: n. pag.

——. "Novela de una novela." *La Fábrica del Sur* 2, June 1990: 17–23.

——. "Objetos encontrados." *ABC literario* 23 July 1988: XVI.

——. *Las otras vidas*. Madrid: Mondadori, 1988.

—— and Luis García Montero. *¿Por qué no es útil la literatura?* Madrid: Ediciones Hiperión, 1993.

——. *Plenilunio*. Madrid: Alfaguara, 1997.

——. *La realidad de la ficción*. Sevilla: Renacimiento, 1993.

——. "El regreso de Lázaro." *El País* 21 July 1990: 22.

——. "El reino de las voces." *ABC literario* 4 Feb. 1989: XVI.

——. *El Robinson urbano*. Pamplona: Pamiela, 1988.

——. "Un santuario para Bill Faulkner." *Quimera* 72 (1987): 50–53.

——. "El secreto de Santiago Biralbo." *El Urogallo* July-Aug.-Sep. 1987: 109.

——. and Ricardo Martín. *Sostener la Mirada. Imágenes de La Alpujarra.* Centro Andaluz de la Fotografía. Junta de Andalucía, 1993.

——. "Teoría del adiós." *ABC* 9 June 1988: n. pag.

——. "La vida breve." *El País* (BABELIA) 11 July 1992: 18–19.

Naharro-Calderón, José María. *Entre el exilio y el interior: el "entresiglo" y Juan Ramón Jiménez.* Barcelona: Anthropos, 1994.

Neruda, Pablo. *Canto general.* Ed. Enrico Mario Santí. Madrid: Cátedra, 1990.

Pérez Galdós, Benito. *Fortunata y Jacinta. I.* Ed. Francisco Caudet. 2nd ed. Madrid: Cátedra, 1985.

——. "Observaciones sobre la novela contemporánea en España." *Revista de España.* 15.57 (1870): 162–72.

Pita, Elena. "Retrato. Antonio Muñoz Molina." *El Mundo* (Magazine) 13–14 June 1992: n. pag.

Place, J.A. and L.S. Peterson. "Some Visual Motifs of Film Noir." *Film Comment* 10.1 (1974): 30–35.

Plett, Heinrich F. "Intertextualities." *Intertextuality.* Ed. Heinrich F. Plett. New York and Berlin: Walter de Gruyter, 1991. 3–29.

Preston, Paul. "Materialism and *Serie Negra*." *Leeds Papers on Thrillers in the Transition. "Novela negra" and Political Change in Spain.* Ed. Rob Rix. Trinity and All Saints College, 1992. 9–16.

Proust, Marcel. *Du côté de chez Swann.* Paris: Gallimard, 1954.

Reyes-Ortiz, Igor. "Muñoz Molina. 'Soy brillante escribiendo'." *Marie Claire* June 1992: 26–30.

Ribas, José. "Antonio Muñoz Molina." *Ajoblanco* May, 1989. 48–55.

Rich, Lawrence. Personal interview with Antonio Muñoz Molina, 16 July 1992.

——. Personal interview with Antonio Muñoz Molina, 24 Aug. 1994.

Riggan, William. *Pícaros, Madmen, Naifs, and Clowns. The Unreliable First-person Narrator.* Norman: University of Oklahoma Press, 1981.

Rignall, John. "Benjamin's *Flâneur* and the Problem of Realism." *The*

Problems of Modernity. Adorno and Benjamin. Ed. Andrew Benjamin. London and New York: Routledge, 1989. 112–21.

Rimmon-Kenan, Shlomith. *Narrative Fiction: Contemporary Poetics*. London and New York: Routledge, 1991.

Rix, Rob, ed. *Leeds Papers on Thrillers in the Transition. "Novela negra" and Political Change in Spain*. Trinity and All Saints College, 1992.

Rodríguez, Emma. "Antonio Muñoz Molina. Una pasión correspondida." *Delibros* 42, February 1992: 36–41.

Rodríguez, Juan María. "La crítica arrastra los tópicos de la progresía." *Diario 16* (Andalucía) 13 March 1989: n. pag.

Salabert, Juana. "Antonio Muñoz Molina califica *El invierno en Lisboa*, su última novela, de 'jam-session'." *El País* 27 May 1987: n. pag.

Sanz Villanueva, Santos. *Historia de la literatura española. El siglo XX. Literatura actual*. 3rd ed. Barcelona: Ariel, 1988.

——. "Una realidad en la última novela española." *Insula* 512–13 (1989): 3–4.

Scholes, Robert. "Metafiction." *Iowa Review* 1.4 (1970): 100–15.

Scholes, Robert and Robert Kellogg. *The Nature of Narrative*. London and New York: Oxford University Press, 1966.

Sebold, Russell P. "'Una lágrima, pero una lágrima sola': Sobre el llanto romántico." *Trayectoria del romanticismo español. Desde la Ilustración hasta Bécquer*. Barcelona: Grijalbo, 1983. 185–94.

Shaw, Donald L. *Historia de la literatura española. El siglo XIX*. Trans. Helena Calsamiglia. 9th ed. Barcelona: Ariel, 1986.

Smith, Barbara Herrnstein. *On the Margins of Discourse. The Relation of Literature to Language*. Chicago and London: The University of Chicago Press, 1978.

Sobejano, Gonzalo. "Ante la novela de los años setenta." *Insula* 396–397 (1979): 1, 22.

——. "Novela y metanovela en España." *Insula* 512–513 (1989): 4–6.

Solana, J. "Entrevista. Antonio Muñoz Molina:...y el jugador sólo mira." *El reportero*. 12 Feb. 1988: VI–VII.

Sorela, Pedro. "Los hijos de Federico Sánchez." *El País* 23 March 1989: 18.

Spires, Robert. *Beyond the Metafictional Mode. Directions in the Modern Spanish Novel*. The University Press of Kentucky, 1984.

——. "El nuevo lenguaje de la 'nueva novela.'" *Insula* 396–397 (1979): 6–7.

Suleiman, Susan. "Introduction: Varieties of Audience-Oriented Criticism." *The Reader in the Text. Essays on Audience and Interpretation*. Ed. Susan R. Suleiman and Inge Crosman. Princeton: Princeton University Press, 1980. 3–45.

Sweeney, S. E. "Locked Rooms: Detective Fiction, Narrative Theory, and Self-Reflexivity." *The Cunning Craft. Original Essays on Detective Fiction and Contemporary Literary Theory*. Ed. Ronald G. Walker and June M. Frazer. Macomb: Western Illinois University, 1990. 1–24.

Tacca, Oscar. *Las voces de la novela*. Madrid: Gredos, 1973.

Tani, Stefano. *The Doomed Detective: The Contribution of the Detective Novel to Postmodern American and Italian Fiction*. Carbondale: Southern Illinois University Press, 1984.

Todorov, Tzvetan. "An Introduction to Verisimilitude." *The Poetics of Prose*. Trans. Richard Howard. Ithaca: Cornell University Press, 1977. 80–88.

——. "Reading as Construction." *The Reader in the Text. Essays on Audience and Interpretation*. Ed. Susan R. Suleiman and Inge Crosman. Princeton: Princeton University Press, 1980. 67–82.

——. "The Typology of Detective Fiction." *The Poetics of Prose*. Trans. Richard Howard. Ithaca: Cornell University Press, 1977. 42–52.

Tuñón de Lara, Manuel, ed. *Historia de España. Tomo X. Transición y democracia (1973–1985)*. Barcelona: Labor, 1992.

Verani, Hugo. *Onetti: el ritual de la impostura*. Caracas: Monte Avila, 1981.

Vidal-Folch, Ignacio. "Muñoz Molina: 'La novela ha de ser útil hasta la obscenidad'." *ABC* 5 March 1989: n. pag.

Vilarós, Teresa M. "Los monos del desencanto español." *Modern Language Notes* 109 (1994): 217–35.

Villanueva, Darío, et al. *Historia y crítica de la literatura española. IX. Los nuevos nombres: 1975–1990*. Ed. Francisco Rico. Barcelona: Editorial Crítica, 1992.

Waugh, Patricia. *Metafiction. The Theory and Practice of Self-Conscious Fiction*. London and New York: Routledge, 1993.

Wellek, René and Austin Warren. *Theory of Literature*. 3rd ed. New York and London: Harcourt Brace Jovanovich, 1977.

White, Hayden. "The Historical Text as Literary Artifact." *Clio* 3.3 (1974): 277–303.

——. "The Value of Narrativity in the Representation of Reality." *The Content of the Form*. Baltimore and London: Johns Hopkins University Press, 1987. 1–25.

Wilde, Alan. *Middle Grounds: Studies in Contemporary American Fiction*. University of Pennsylvania Press, 1987.

Wilson, Edmund. "Who Cares Who Killed Roger Ackroyd?" *Detective Fiction: A Collection of Critical Essays*. Ed. Robin W. Winks. Englewood Cliffs, NJ: Prentice Hall, 1980. 35–40.

Wimsatt, William K. *The Verbal Icon: Studies in the Meaning of Poetry*. Lexington: University of Kentucky Press, 1954.

Zavala, Iris M. "Costumbrismo y novelas." *Historia y crítica de la literatura española. Tomo V. Romanticismo y realismo*. Ed. Francisco Rico. Barcelona: Grijalbo, 1982. 337–48.

Index

ABC, 1
Abrams, M. H., 11
Alberti, Rafael, 37
Alonso, Santos, 3, 105, 107, 115
Alter, Robert, 6, 43
Amell, Samuel, 105
"amor imposible, Un," 61–62
Amorós, Andrés, 3
Ardor guerrero, xii, 8, 116
"Arte nuevo de escribir novelas," 16
autobiographical pact, 101–103
autobiography, xii, 8, 92, 95, 98–99, 101–102
autoreferentiality, 107

Barthes, Roland, 23, 58–60, 62–63
Baudelaire, Charles, 11–12, 72
Beatus ille, 1, 5, 7–8, 16, 18, 21, 27, 29, 36–47, 49–53, 62, 64, 65, 67–72, 80–81, 85–86, 95, 99–100, 106, 112
Beltenebros, 1, 5, 7, 9n, 16, 18, 29, 36–39, 41–43, 47–52, 64, 72, 80, 86, 100, 106
Benveniste, Emile, 22–23
Bermúdez, Silvia, xii
bildungsroman, 82, 85
biography, 95, 101–102
Booth, Wayne, 31n, 54n
Borges, Jorge Luis, 7, 10n, 86–87

"Borrador de una historia," 50–51, 72–73
bosque de Diana, El, 1
Brown, Joan Lipman, 107
"Byron, the wanderer," 98

"cara del pasado, La" 82
Casablanca, 30, 83–85
Castellet, José María, 2
Cawelti, John, 81, 87
Cervantes, Miguel de, 1, 12, 79–80
Chandler, Raymond, 7–8, 79, 81, 87
Cien años de soledad (García Márquez), 97, 117n
Civil War, Spanish, 2, 5, 6–7, 9n, 49, 111–112
Cohn, Dorrit, 101–102
Coleridge, Samuel, 12
"colina de los sacrificios, La," 13, 23, 26, 31
Compitello, Malcolm, xi
Córdoba de los omeyas, 1
"Correspondencia," 12
Cortázar, Julio, 7, 53
costumbrismo, 87–92
crime novel. *See* detective novel.
cuadro de costumbres, 87–88; parody of, 88–89
"Cuando Onetti," 31n
"cuarto del fantasma, El," 21

Culler, Jonathan, 23
cutting. *See* reader response

"Decadencia del crimen," 114
deictics, 23
"desencanto, el," 4–5, 7–8, 10n, 111–116
"Desocupado lector," 8, 58
detective fiction, 65, 80
detective novel, 7, 66–67, 81; formal, 65–66, 68, 85–87; hard-boiled, 65, 81, 85–87
"detectives, Los," 7, 93n
Diario de Granada (newspaper), 1, 9n
Diario del Nautilus, 12, 18, 78–80, 106, 114
doubles, use of, 51–52, 72–73, 87
dueño del secreto, El, xii, 6, 8, 16, 29, 92, 101–108, 115
Durán Manuel, 6

Eco, Umberto, 3, 84
"edad de la novela, La," 65, 114
Eliot, T. S., 19
epistemology, xi, 7, 8, 114

"Fábula de Fuentes," 7
Faulkner, William, 25, 81
feuilleton. *See folletín*
fiction, 100–101, 116; pulp, 48, 50, 89–90; and history, 35, 97
film, 30, 48–49, 80–82
film noir, 8, 49, 71, 81–82, 85, 94n
first-person narration. *See* narrator
flâneur, 73
Flaubert, Gustave, 85
focalization, narrative, 23, 26–28, 32n, 44–45, 50–51, 70
Foley, Barbara, 101
folletín, 8, 21–22, 29, 40, 80–81, 87, 91, 95–96

Fortunata y Jacinta (Pérez Galdós), 22, 46
Foucault, Michel, 77–78
Freund, Elizabeth, 57, 74
Frye, Northrop, 57

Galán Lorés, Carlos, 3
García Lorca, Federico, 79
García Márquez, Gabriel, 7, 97
García-Moreno Barco, Francisco, xi, 9n
Garvey, Diane, 107
Genette, Gérard, 74
"gentileza de los desconocidos, La," 65
Goytisolo, Juan, 2, 3, 5, 36
Goytisolo, Luis, 6
Grella, George, 66
Guelbenzu, José María, 5

Hammet, Dashiell, 7–8, 81
hermeneutic code. *See* reader response
Hernández, Miguel, 37, 44
Herrnstein Smith, Barbara, 101
Herzberger, David, 5–6, 8, 36
history, 6, 39, 41–42; vs. discourse, 22; and fiction, 35, 43, 97, 101, 103
Hitchcock, Alfred, 81, 85
"hombre sombra, El," 14–15, 21, 71
Hühn, Peter, 66–67
Hutcheon, Linda, 43, 49–50, 65, 79, 107

imagination, 6, 12–16, 18–22, 24–27, 29–30, 40–43, 46, 51, 70–71, 82, 92, 116; and reader response, 58, 71, 95–96, 100–101, 103–105
indeterminacy. *See* reader response
intertextuality, xii, 7, 20, 77–92, 106; definitions of, 77–78; generic, 80,

85; and film, 81–85; parodic, 78–79; and the reader, 79–80, 85–87

invierno en Lisboa, El, 1, 8, 16, 18, 24–30, 45, 58–59, 64–65, 71, 81–86, 100, 106

Iser, Wolfgang, 8, 57–59, 62–63, 71–74

Jakobson, Roman, 9n, 57
Jauss, Hans Robert, 74, 80
Jiménez, Juan Ramón, 106
jinete polaco, El, xii, 1, 6, 8, 16–21, 27–29, 31n, 62, 65, 72–73, 80, 90, 92, 95–97, 100, 102–103, 105–108, 112–114, 116
Joyce, James, 79, 85
"Juego de las conmemoraciones," 20

Labanyi, Jo, 36
Landero, Luis, 3
Lanser, Susan, 23, 31n
Larra, Mariano José de, 88–89
"Lecciones de abismo," 99
"Lectura y adicción," 80
Lejeune, Philippe, 101–103
Lévi-Strauss, Claude, 57
Lezama Lima, José, 78–79
"libros y los trenes, Los," 12
Llamazares, Julio, 54n
Lodge, David, 44, 59–60
López Guerra, Luis, 111
"lugar donde vivir, Un," 98
"Luna de los escaparates," 79–80

Madrid, Juan, 3, 7
Mainer, José Carlos, 4, 7, 37
"maleficio de los nombres, El," 106
Maltese Falcon, The, 86
"manera de vivir, La," 18, 40

"mano de nieve, La," 18
"mantequeros de Perú, Los," 60
"máquinas del tiempo, Las," 18
Marsé, Juan, 5, 8, 107
Martín, Andreu, 7
Martín Gaite, Carmen, 5, 8, 107
Martín-Santos, Luis, 2
Martínez Reverte, Jorge, 7
mask, narrative, 98–101, 103
Mateo Díez, Luis, 5
Matute, Ana María, 5
McHale, Brian, xi
melodrama, 80, 87
"memoria en donde ardía, La," 78
memory, 6, 11, 16–21, 24–27, 29, 41–43, 46, 70–71, 82, 92, 95–96, 100–101, 103–104, 116
Mendoza, Eduardo, 3
Mesonero Romanos, Ramón de, 88–89
metafiction, xii, 6–8, 30, 43–44, 47, 66, 70, 72, 105–108, 114; *Beatus ille* as, 85–86; *Beltenebros* as, 49, 87; historiographic, 49–50; *El invierno en Lisboa* as, 71, 84; *El jinete polaco* as, 107; *Los misterios de Madrid* as, 91; vs. realism, 106–108
Millás, Juan José, 6
"mirada que pinta, La," 91
mise en abîme, in *Beltenebros*, 49, 87
misterios de Madrid, Los, 8, 21, 27–29, 55n, 63–65, 87–91, 112–113,
modernism vs. postmodernism, xi
Montero, Rosa, 3
Montesinos, José, 88
Morales Cuesta, Manuel María, xii
myth, in postwar fiction, 36

"Nada del otro mundo" (short story), 5

Nada del otro mundo (anthology), 12–14, 31n, 51, 61–62, 65, 70–73
narrativization, 35
narratology, xii
narrator: first-person, 20–22, 24, 26–28, 31n, 32n, 45–47, 87, 103–104; heterodiegetic, 28, 33n; homodiegetic, 22, 24, 29, 31n, 44–45; omniscient, 22–24, 45, 68; realist, 21–22; third-person, 21–24, 26–29, 32, 46, 47, 50, 68; unreliable, 22, 31n, 32n, 97, 107
neorealism, 114; reaction against, 6
neorrealismo, 2
Neruda, Pablo, 38
nostalgia, 88, 115–116
"Noticia de una tentativa," 21, 81, 98
novel: autobiographical, 102; crime, 65; detective, 7, 65–67, 81; experimental, 3; of memory, 5, 16, 36; metafictional, 6, 43; neorealist, 3, 10; self-conscious, 6, 43; of social realism, 2; of the transition, 3
novela de entregas, 63
"Novela de una novela," 58
novela negra, 7, 81–82, 85, 93n, 115

"Objetos encontrados," 17
Oleza, Juan, 4, 105
Onetti, Juan Carlos, 7, 15
Ortíz, Lourdes, 5
otras vidas, Las, 16, 21

País, El, 1, 63, 91, 105
parody, 78–79; of *costumbrismo*, 88–90
PCE (Spanish Communist Party), 38
Pérez Galdós, Benito, 12, 21–22
picaresque novel, 32n
Piquer, Concha, 79
Plenilunio, xii

Plett, Heinrich, 77, 79–80
Poema de Mío Cid, 35
¿Por qué no es útil la literatura?, 9n
"poseída, La," 12–13, 23, 26, 31n, 70
postmodernism, xi; and irony, 84
Preston, Paul, 7, 10
proairetic code. *See* reader response
Proust, Marcel, 6, 17
PSOE (Spanish Socialist Workers Party), 4, 112

Quevedo, Francisco de, 78–79

reader: active, 53; of autobiography, 101–102; inscribed, 70–73, 77; real vs. implied, 73–74
reader reception, xii
reader response, xii, 8, 57; and cutting, 62–64, 87; and indeterminacy, 58–59, 70–71, 73, 77; and proairetic code, 59–60, 65; and hermeneutic code, 59–60, 62–66; contrasted with reader reception, 74
realidad de la ficción, La, 9, 12–13, 18, 21, 24, 32, 29–30, 65, 100, 116
realism, 105–107; definition of, 9n; and first-person narration, 22; self-conscious, 8, 95, 105, 107, 116; social, 2, 49; vs. metafiction, 106–108
realismo social, 2
"regreso de Lázaro, El," 60–61
"reino de las voces, El," 11, 21, 80
Rimmon-Kenan, Shlomith, 59, 67–69, 74
Robinson urbano, El, 9, 12, 13, 20, 46, 72–73, 78–79, 98
romanticism, 11, 90

"santuario para Bill Faulkner, Un," 32n

Sanz Villanueva, Santos, 2, 3, 9n, 115
Sautier Casaseca, Guillermo, 80
"secreto de Santiago Biralbo, El," 59
self-conscious novel: definition of, 43; *Beltenebros* as a, 49
self-conscious realism, 8, 95, 105, 107, 116
self-referentiality. *See* self-reflexivity
self-reflexivity, 3, 8, 51, 106; detective story and, 65–67
Semprún, Jorge, 5
"Septiembre escueto y rosa," 78–79
Sobejano, Gonzalo, 6
Sostener la Mirada. Imágenes de la Alpujarra, 20
Spanish Civil War. *See* Civil War
Spires, Robert, 3, 47

"Te golpearé sin cólera," 64
"Teoría del adiós," 13
third-person narration. *See* narrator
Todorov, Tzvetan, 66
"Todos los fuegos, el fuego" (Muñoz Molina) 9

Ulysses (Joyce), 85

Vázquez Montalbán, Manuel, 3, 7
verisimilitude, 22, 31n, 54n, 68, 95, 100–101, 107
"vida breve, La," 31n
Vilarós, Teresa, 4, 10
"voz y el estilo, La," 24

Waugh, Patricia, 44, 107
White, Hayden, 13, 35

Currents in Comparative Romance Languages and Literatures

This series was founded in 1987, and actively solicits book-length manuscripts (approximately 200–400 pages) which treat aspects of Romance Languages and Literatures. Originally established for works dealing with two or more Romance literatures, the series has broadened its horizons and now includes studies on themes within a single literature or between different literatures, civilizations, art, music, film and social movements, as well as comparative linguistics. Studies on individual writers with an influence on other literatures/civilizations are also welcome. We entertain a variety of approaches and formats, provided the scholarship and methodology are appropriate.

For additional information about the series or for the submission of manuscripts, please contact:

>Tamara Alvarez-Detrell and Michael G. Paulson
>c/o Dr. Heidi Burns
>Peter Lang Publishing, Inc.
>516 N. Charles St., 2nd Floor
>Baltimore, MD 21201

OHIO UNIVERSITY LIBRARY